Egoism and Altruism

Basic Problems in Philosophy Series

A. I. Melden and Stanley Munsat
University of California, Irvine
General Editors

Ethical Relativism
John Ladd, Brown University

Human Rights
A. I. Melden

Egoism and Altruism
Ronald D. Milo, University of Arizona

Guilt and Shame
Herbert Morris, University of California, Los Angeles

The Analytic-Synthetic Distinction
Stanley Munsat

Civil Disobedience and Violence
Jeffrie G. Murphy, University of Arizona

Morality and the Law
Richard A. Wasserstrom, University of California, Los Angeles

War and Morality
Richard A. Wasserstrom

Egoism and Altruism

edited by

RONALD D. MILO
University of Arizona

Wadsworth Publishing Company, Inc.
Belmont, California

Design: Gary A. Head

Editing: Sandra Craig

Cover: Steve Renick

ISBN 0-534-00280-3

L. C. Cat. Card No. 72-97321

Printed in the United States of America

1 2 3 4 5 6 7 8 9 10—77 76 75 74 73

To keep the price of this book as low as possible, we have used an economical means of typesetting. We welcome your comments.

Series Foreword

The Basic Problems in Philosophy Series is designed to meet the need of students and teachers of philosophy, mainly but not exclusively at the undergraduate level, for collections of essays devoted to some fairly specific philosophical problems.

In recent years there have been numerous paperback collections on a variety of philosophical topics. Those teachers who wish to refer their students to a set of essays on a specific philosophical problem have usually been frustrated, however, since most of these collections range over a wide set of issues and problems. The present series attempts to remedy this situation by presenting together, within each volume, key writings on a single philosophical issue.

Given the magnitude of the literature, there can be no thought of completeness. Rather, the materials included are those that, in the judgment of the editor, must be mastered first by the student who wishes to acquaint himself with relevant issues and their ramifications. To this end, historical as well as contemporary writings are included.

Each volume in the series contains an introduction by the editor to set the stage for the arguments contained in the essays and a bibliography to help the student who wishes to pursue the topic at a more advanced level.

A. I. Melden
S. Munsat

Contents

Introduction

Perhaps no issue is more central in moral philosophy than that concerning the relative merits of the claims made upon our conduct by our self-interest and by the interests of others. Debate has centered not only on the question of the extent to which each of these claims ought to govern our conduct but also on the question of the extent to which each of them actually does govern our conduct. The term 'egoism' is most often used as a label either for the view that people ought to act in such a way as to best promote their own interests, subordinating the demands made upon their conduct by the interests of others to this primary concern (*ethical egoism*), or for the view that people do in fact always act in such a way as to make the pursuit of their own interests their primary and overriding concern (*psychological egoism*).

EGOISM AS A TRAIT OF CHARACTER

However, there is also a third sense in which the term 'egoism' may be used. When contrasted with 'altruism' it is often used to indicate a trait of character that consists of an exclusive concern with one's own interests, in the sense that one is willing to promote the interests or welfare of others only insofar as this is considered conducive to promoting one's own interests, and is willing to sacrifice the interests of others (even to harm them) when this is considered instrumental to promoting or safeguarding one's own interests. Such a character trait is also called selfishness. Altruism, on the other hand, is usually equated with unselfishness, with a direct or uncalculated concern for the interests of others. Thus, in this sense of the term, an *egoist*, as contrasted with an altruist, is a selfish person. He is basically self-centered and indifferent to the welfare of others. Sometimes the term 'egotism' is also used in this sense—i.e., as a synonym for

1

'selfishness'—but most often it is used to indicate a somewhat
different trait of character—that of vanity or conceit in general and boastfulness and excessive self-reference in particular. An egotist in the latter sense need not be, though he
probably will be, selfish.
     Selfishness is considered by most of us to be a bad char-
acter trait, a vice, whereas unselfishness is generally considered to be a virtue. Indeed, many consider selfishness to be
the very essence of immorality and consider unselfishness to be
the principal moral virtue. Thus, while egoism is widely condemned as immoral, altruism is commended as a virtue. But if
this is so, how shall we conceive of altruism? If eogism is
conceived of as including a disposition to sacrifice the interests of others for the sake of our own (to treat others as mere
means to our own happiness), shall we then conceive of altruism
as including a disposition to sacrifice our own interests for
the sake of others (to treat ourselves as mere means to the
happiness of others)?[1] If we conceive of altruism in this way,
as involving self-renunciation and self-abasement, it can be
argued that altruism is far from a virtue and more like a vice.
As A. C. Ewing observes:

> A society in which everybody spent his life sacri-
> ficing all his pleasure for others would be even more
> absurd than a society whose members all lived by
> taking in each other's washing. In a society of such
> completely unselfish people who would be prepared to
> accept and benefit by the sacrifice? And the purpose-
> less surrender of one's happiness is mere folly.[2]

For this reason Ewing suggests that if altruism is to be considered a virtue, it must be conceived of differently: "Self-sacrifice is only required . . . where it is necessary in order to
secure for somebody else a *greater* good than that sacrificed."
Thus, the altruist is to be characterized not as one who puts
the interests of others ahead of his own but as one who puts
the interests of others on an equal footing with his own.
     However, even this characterization of altruism would not
convince everyone that altruism is a virtue. First, there are
those who claim that altruism so characterized—as consisting
of a direct, uncalculated concern for the interests of others—

---

[1]It is interesting to note that one recent defender of "the
virtue of selfishness" does conceive of altruism in this way.
Cf. Ayn Rand, *The Virtue of Selfishness* (New York: Signet
Books, 1964), especially essays 1 and 5.

[2]A. C. Ewing, *Ethics* (New York: Collier Books, 1962), p. 34.

is impossible. Human beings are so constituted, it is held, that the pursuit of their own interests is always their primary aim and—in cases where this conflicts with the interests of others—their overriding concern. This is the thesis of *psychological egoism*. Insofar as being altruistic requires us to intentionally sacrifice our own interests "in order to secure for somebody else a *greater* good than that sacrificed," it requires what is psychologically impossible. Psychological egoism, in other words, maintains that selfishness (egoism as a state of character) is a universal character trait.

Second, there are those who claim that even if altruism so characterized were possible, it could hardly be commended as a virtue. For, it has been maintained, it can never be reasonable for a man to intentionally act contrary to his genuine self-interest. If being altruistic requires one to make a genuine sacrifice of one's self-interest, then it requires one to act in a manner contrary to reason. And a disposition to act in such a manner can hardly be considered a virtue. This view—that it cannot be reasonable for a man to intentionally act contrary to his own self-interest—is, as we shall see, closely associated with the thesis of *ethical egoism*—the view that one ought always to act in such a way as will best promote one's own interests in the long run. According to ethical egoism, it is false to maintain that one ought to put the interests of others on an equal footing with one's own; rather, the demands made upon one's conduct by the interests of others ought always to be made subordinate to the demands of one's own long-range self-interest.

Let us now consider each of these two theses—psychological egoism and ethical egoism—in more detail.

PSYCHOLOGICAL EGOISM

It has become customary among philosophers to apply the label 'psychological egoism' to any theory of human motivation which implies (or is thought by its proponents to imply) that human beings are basically selfish in character and that no voluntary human actions are ever genuinely unselfish or purely altruistic.[3] The most extreme forms of psychological egoism would be those theories which imply that human beings have *no* direct concern or desire for the good of others, which imply,

---

[3]However, to deny that actions are ever genuinely unselfish is not to claim that all actions are selfish. Not all actions must be characterized as either selfish or unselfish. For example, brushing one's teeth would be neither selfish nor unselfish in normal circumstances.

in other words, that no human being is ever motivated to act by a concern for the good of another as an end in itself. A more moderate kind of psychological egoism would be a theory of motivation which allows that human beings do have *some* concern for the good of others as an end in itself but implies that a concern for one's own good always outweighs, in motivational strength, a concern for the good of others.

Egoistic theories of motivation can also be divided into those that are monistic in character and those that are pluralistic. Theories are monistic if they claim that there is only one kind of ultimate motive, all other motives being in some way subordinate to or derivative from this one. Theories of this sort commonly assume this ultimate motive to be the desire for one's own happiness (or sometimes the desire for self-preservation). Very often self-love or self-interest is thought to be such a motive. Pluralistic versions of psychological egoism allow that there are a number of ultimate, irreducible motives of conduct but insist that all such motives are to be characterized as egoistic—in the sense that human actions having any one of these as their ultimate motive (or motives) could not be said to be genuinely unselfish or altruistic.

Perhaps the most persuasive kind of monistic psychological egoism is that which claims that "the only kind of ultimate desire is the desire to get or prolong pleasant experiences, and to avoid or cut short unpleasant experiences, for oneself."[4] The term 'psychological hedonism' is often used as a label for this form of psychological egoism. But the term 'psychological hedonism' is also sometimes applied more broadly to any theory of motivation that assigns to pleasure and pain a decisive role in the determination of human conduct (which maintains, as Bentham put it, that "nature has placed mankind under the governance of two sovereign masters, *pain* and *pleasure*"). In this broader sense of the term, psychological hedonism is not *by definition* a species of psychological egoism, although one could debate whether every theory of motivation that is hedonistic in this sense is also egoistic.

It is important to recognize this point about the broader sense in which the term 'psychological hedonism' may be employed, since a failure to do so may lead to confusion and a begging of the question at issue—i.e., the question of whether all hedonistic theories of motivation are also egoistic. Yet this point has been overlooked. C. D. Broad, for example, describes psychological hedonism as "the doctrine that my volitions are determined wholly and solely by my pleasures and pains, present and prospective," and then immediately (in the

---

[4]C. D. Broad, "Egoism as a Theory of Human Motives," p. 88 of this volume.

next sentence) says: "It is thus a particular species of
Psychological Egoism."[5] Broad concludes from this that any
refutation of psychological egoism would ipso facto be a refutation of psychological hedonism. Conversely, this leads one
to think that if one affirms psychological hedonism in this
broad sense (excuse the pun), he thereby affirms an egoistic
theory of motivation. This is quite misleading.

In its broader sense, the term 'psychological hedonism'
is applicable to at least three different types of theories of
motivation. The first of these is sometimes called "psychological hedonism of the future."[6] This theory conforms to the
narrower definition of psychological hedonism as the doctrine
that "the only kind of ultimate desire is the desire to get or
prolong pleasant experiences, and to avoid or cut short unpleasant experiences, for oneself." This type of psychological
hedonism does appear to be egoistic, since it holds that obtaining or maintaining pleasant experiences for oneself and
avoiding or terminating painful experiences for oneself form
one's only ultimate goal.

But there is another type of psychological hedonism, sometimes called "psychological hedonism of the present," which is
not so obviously egoistic. This theory holds that a person
will be motivated to act so as to bring about a certain state
of affairs if and only if he finds the thought of that state of
affairs pleasant, and he will be motivated to act so as to
avoid a certain state of affairs if and only if he finds the
thought of that state painful.

This is the sort of theory defended by Moritz Schlick, yet
he vehemently denies that it is proper to call his theory egoistic.[7] Schlick's fundamental "law of motivation" is "that one
can act only toward that end whose idea is most pleasant for
one." His theory is to be distinguished from "psychological
hedonism of the future" (which we might also label 'egoistic
psychological hedonism') because (1) he distinguishes between
the *pleasant idea of a state* and the *idea of a pleasant state*
(his theory employs the former notion), and (2) he does not
insist that the prevailing pleasant idea be of one's personal
condition. Since there is no reason why the thought of some
state of affairs which would be pleasant for others but not for
oneself (and which might even be painful for oneself) might not

[5]C. D. Broad, *Five Types of Ethical Theory* (London: Routledge
and Kegan Paul, 1956), pp. 180–81.

[6]Cf. R. B. Brandt, *Ethical Theory* (Englewood Cliffs, N.J.:
Prentice-Hall, 1959), pp. 307–14.

[7]See the selection from Schlick's "Problems of Ethics" in this
volume, p. 75.

be a pleasant thought for oneself, there is some doubt as to whether we should call such a theory egoistic.

A third type of psychological hedonism, "psychological hedonism of the past," is that suggested by certain recent psychologists. This theory holds that one's present motives (or at least the strength of them) are a function of one's previous conditioning by pleasant and painful (or unpleasant) experiences. Thus, whether one now prefers (or is motivated to choose) A rather than B is determined by the fact that in the past the experience of A was on the whole more pleasant than that of B. Here again, since one's previous pleasant experiences might cause one now to choose a state of affairs that one believes to be pleasant for others but not for oneself, there is some question about calling this theory egoistic.

It is important to draw another distinction which has generally been overlooked in discussions of psychological egoism. In the *Leviathan* Thomas Hobbes gives two formulations of psychological egoism: (1) "Of the voluntary acts of every man, the object is *some good to himself*"; (2) "Of all voluntary acts, the object is to every man *his own good*."[8]   These two formulations of psychological egoism are open to quite different interpretations. The latter formulation suggests that in his voluntary actions each man does what he thinks will bring about the greatest balance of good over evil for himself. It suggests, in other words, that men are by nature prudent, that they always do what they think will be best for themselves on the whole. Hobbes's position is sometimes interpreted in this way. For example, R. B. Brandt describes the thesis of psychological egoism as follows (I shall divide it into two parts):

> The thesis asserts (like Hobbes . . .) that [a] a person is motivated to produce a certain situation if and only if he believes it will be, or produce, a desirable state of himself; and [b] he will be motivated to produce one situation in preference to another if and only if he believes it will be, or produce, on balance, a more desirable state of himself.[9]

What I have labeled part [a] of Brandt's formulation of the thesis is, taken by itself, one way of interpreting Hobbes's first formulation (1). We might call this an assertion of *weak* psychological egoism. If we conjoin parts [a] and [b] of

[8]See his *Leviathan*. The first formulation occurs in chap. 14 and the second in chap. 15 of that work. Italics in the second quotation are mine.

[9]R. B. Brandt, *Ethical Theory*, p. 371.

Brandt's formulation, we have an interpretation of Hobbes's second formulation (2). We might call this an assertion of *strong* psychological egoism.

That these two theses are quite different can be shown by constructing a case whose existence would be compatible with the truth of weak psychological egoism but not with the truth of strong psychological egoism. Suppose a man is advised by his physician that, for the sake of his health—say, to ward off the dangers of heart disease—he must restrict his diet by avoiding foods high in cholesterol. And suppose that he accepts this as sound advice. It may happen, however, that the foods he is supposed to avoid are just those foods he is most fond of. Because of this, he may sometimes violate his dietary prescription. When he does eat these forbidden foods, he is motivated by a desire for something which he believes to be, in some respect, good or desirable for himself. For he does think that these foods have a very pleasant taste, and he considers this fact at least *a* (though not a *conclusive*) reason for preferring such foods and for judging them desirable and good to eat. However, he does not believe that eating such foods is good or desirable on the whole (all things considered), for he accepts his physician's advice as sound.

Cases such as this, in which a person intentionally acts contrary to his judgment of what is better or best for himself, all things considered, have been described as cases of weakness of will. What I am calling "strong psychological egoism" implies not only that genuine altruism is impossible but also that weakness of will is impossible. Philosophers who want to defend strong, rather than weak, psychological egoism will thus have a much more difficult task, for most philosophers would claim that to deny the possibility of weakness of will is to deny a plain matter of fact. Thus, Joseph Butler thinks it obvious that "mankind have ungoverned passions which they will gratify at any rate, as well as to the injury of others, as in contradiction to known private interest."[10]

ETHICAL EGOISM

As was mentioned earlier, many philosophers have claimed that even if it is psychologically possible for a man to act contrary to his own interests, it cannot be reasonable for him to do so. Unlike psychological egoism, this view concerns the *justification*, rather than the *explanation*, of human conduct. It is a thesis not about how men do act or why they act as they

[10]Joseph Butler, *Fifteen Sermons* (London: G. Bell and Sons, 1953), p. 42. Cf. also p. 25 of this volume.

do but about how men *ought* to act. When stated more positively, as the view that one ought always to act in the way that will best promote one's own interests or good on the whole, it is often called 'ethical egoism'. If one believes that it cannot be reasonable for a man to intentionally act contrary to his own interests on the whole, and if one also believes that what morality requires us to do must always be reasonable, then one will naturally conclude that morality cannot really require us ever to sacrifice our genuine, long-range interests. The conjunction of these two premises yields a negative version of ethical egoism—namely, that it is right (in the sense of being permissible or not wrong) for each man to act in such a way as will best promote his own interests on the whole.

This is the version of ethical egoism Hobbes seems to defend. Indeed, it is just another way of formulating Hobbes's "Right of Nature," in defense of which Hobbes appeals both to psychological egoism and to the thesis (which he thinks follows logically from psychological egoism) that it cannot be *unreasonable* for a man to act in such a way as will best promote his own interests on the whole:[11]

> And forasmuch as necessity of nature maketh men to will and desire *bonum sibi*, that which is good for themselves, and to avoid that which is hurtful; but most of all, the terrible enemy of nature, death, from whom we expect both the loss of all power, and all the greatest of bodily pains in the losing; it is not against reason, that a man doth all that he can to preserve his own body and limbs both from death and pain. And that which is not against reason, men call *right*, or *jus*, or *blameless liberty* of using our natural power and ability. It is therefore a right of nature, that every man may preserve his own life and limbs with all the power he hath.[12]

This version of ethical egoism is, however, much weaker than that expressed by the positive formulation, which holds that it is not merely permissible or reasonable but that one ought (it is obligatory) to act so as to best promote one's own interests on the whole, and which holds, moreover, that this is

---

[11]Notice that this is not the same as the thesis we have just been considering—i.e., it cannot be *reasonable* for a man to act contrary to his own interests on the whole—although Hobbes would no doubt affirm the latter as well.

[12]Thomas Hobbes, *The Elements of Law (De Corpore Politico)*, chap. 1, paragraph 6.

one's ultimate and overriding moral obligation. It is important to distinguish these two versions (even though most textbook writers have failed to do so) because they are logically
distinct views. Nevertheless, it is quite natural to take the
step from the negative (weaker) version to the positive
(stronger) version. If one believes that it cannot be reasonable to intentionally act contrary to one's self-interest, one
might naturally conclude that one ought not to act contrary to
one's self-interest. For it may seem obvious that one ought
not to do that which it is unreasonable to do, and that if it
can never be reasonable (in accordance with reason) to intentionally act contrary to one's self-interest, it must always
be unreasonable (contrary to reason) to do so. But if one
ought never to intentionally act in a manner contrary to one's
self-interest, then it seems that what one ought to do is to
always act so as to best promote one's self-interest.

Thus, the argument in favor of ethical egoism, in either
of its formulations, is quite powerful and persuasive. Those
who attack it must be prepared to challenge either the claim
that it can never be reasonable to intentionally act contrary
to one's own long-range interests or the claim that morality
can never require us to do what it is unreasonable (in the
sense of being contrary to reason) to do.

Although few philosophers have been willing to challenge
the second of these claims, a number of them have challenged
the first claim. Immanuel Kant, for example, thought it a
mistake to suppose that one's reasons for action were always
constituted by one's interests or inclinations. He believed
this to be a totally inadequate conception of practical reason,
of what it is in accordance with or contrary to reason to do.
And if reasons for action were restricted to reasons of this
sort, morality might very well require us to act in a manner
contrary to reason. But reasons for action are not all of this
sort. Kant believed that the mere fact that an action is one's
duty provides one with a reason for doing it—independently of
what one's interests or inclinations are. Thus, if, as may
sometimes be the case, it is our duty to do something which we
believe to be contrary to our self-interest, it does not follow
that it would be contrary to reason to perform our moral duty.
Rather, since moral reasons always take precedence over prudential ones, it would be contrary to reason not to perform our
duty.

A similar line of argument was taken by H. A. Prichard.
In attacking the position of the ethical egoist—"that it is
impossible for an action to be really . . . a duty, unless it
is for the advantage of the agent"—he saw correctly that the
basic premise to be challenged is "that in the last resort
there is one, and only one, reason why we ought to do anything
whatever, *viz.* the conduciveness to our own happiness or

advantage."[13]   But this last claim, Prichard contended, rests
on a fundamental mistake concerning the nature of practical
reason and human motivation.   The mistake is to suppose that
psychological egoism is true, to suppose that "desire for some
good to oneself is the only motive of deliberate action."[14]
The claim to be challenged rests on this supposition together
with the belief that reasons for action must be capable of mo-
tivating us.   Prichard saw psychological egoism, so formulated,
as having two negative implications:

> The first is that the thought, or alternately, the
> knowledge, that some action is right has no influ-
> ence on us in acting, i.e. that the thought, or the
> knowledge, that an action is a duty can neither be
> our motive nor even an element in our motive.
>   The second implication is that there is no such
> thing as a *desire* to do what is right, or more fully,
> a desire to do some action in virtue of its being a
> duty.[15]

Whereas Kant attempted to attack the first of these implications, Prichard attacked the second.   Prichard attempted to
convince us both that such a desire exists and that it cannot
be identified with or reduced to "desire for some good to
oneself."
    Prichard's attack on ethical egoism makes clear why moral
philosophers have been concerned to challenge the truth of psychological egoism.   They have seen an important logical connection between psychological and ethical egoism and have found it
necessary in challenging the former to attack the latter as
well.   For this reason the readings that compose this anthology
focus primarily, but not exclusively, on the topic of psychological egoism.   However, although it is true that most of the
selections do have a greater bearing on the topic of psychological rather than ethical egoism, the real focus of this volume
is on neither psychological nor ethical egoism but on the fundamental concepts that must be mastered and clarified before we
can be in a position to assess either of these theses.   Before
we can determine whether either of them is true, we must first
come to terms with concepts such as egoistic, selfishness,
self-interest, altruistic, benevolence, and sympathy.

---

[13]H. A. Prichard, "Duty and Interest," in Sellars and Hospers,
eds. *Readings in Ethical Theory* (New York: Appleton—Century-
Crofts, 1952), pp. 473, 474.

[14]Ibid., p. 484.

[15]Ibid.

EGOISM, SELFISHNESS, AND SELF-INTEREST

The readings from Hobbes, Butler, Schlick, Broad, and Michael Slote have been selected because of the contributions they make toward our understanding of what it means to claim that actions are egoistic, selfish, or done out of self-interest. The reader should keep in mind a number of questions regarding these concepts in studying these selections. For example, what is the relationship between selfishness and self-interest (or self-love)? Is to act out of self-interest always to act selfishly? When I put something away for a rainy day (make provision for sickness or retirement) I act out of a concern for my own interests. Do I also act out of self-interest? Do I act selfishly? What about the cases in which I have my appendix removed or give up smoking? Suppose I do not do these things? Do I then act contrary to my own self-interest? Is self-interest (or self-love) a particular kind of motive? Is to act out of self-interest to pursue a peculiar kind of goal, or is it to pursue whatever goals one has in particular ways? Is to claim that a man acted out of self-interest to ascribe to him a particular motive, or is it rather to level a charge or accusation against him—to deny that he acted from a worthy motive?

What is the relationship between one's self-interest and one's interests? One's interests, we may say, include the things one is interested in or enjoys doing. But does it follow that if one is interested in something (e.g., gambling), it is therefore in one's interest? Conversely, does it follow from the fact that it is in one's interest to do something (e.g., to lose weight) that one is therefore interested in doing it? These are only some of the questions that we must be able to answer if we are to master the concepts involved.

No one is more responsible for arousing the interest of philosophers in such concepts as these than Thomas Hobbes. His espousal of psychological egoism (his so-called selfish hypothesis) was a tremendous stimulus for much of the profound and subtle thinking (on the part of Butler, David Hume, and others) concerning the nature of self-love and of its relationships to benevolence and morality. Hobbes' assertion, "Of the voluntary acts of every man, the object is some *good to himself*," is one of the most succinct formulations of psychological egoism ever produced. And, as we have already noted, Hobbes employed this as a key premise in his argument for ethical egoism.

But although Hobbes was responsible for stimulating much of the interest in understanding such concepts as self-love, self-interest, and selfishness, it was Butler who made the most noteworthy contributions to their philosophical analysis. His painstaking attempt to lay bare the conceptual confusions which he thought lay at the basis of Hobbes's position have come to

be recognized as a monumental philosophical achievement for
which philosophers will be forever indebted to him. Because
Butler's important observations are expressed in an archaic
language that, together with their extreme subtlety, make them
difficult to grasp, it may be useful to outline the most important of them for the reader.

(1) Butler first points out that we must distinguish between self-love, which he defines as a general desire of one's
own happiness, and "a variety of particular affections, passions, and appetites" that may also motivate any man. He distinguishes between these in terms of their objects. The object
of self-love "is somewhat internal, our own happiness, enjoyment, satisfaction." The objects of our particular desires
"are this or that particular external thing." For example, the
object of hunger is food (or, rather, eating food), that of
fear is some particular harm or danger (which it prompts us to
avoid), and that of lust is an act of sexual intercourse.
While both the particular desires and the general desire for
one's own happiness (self-love) are constitutive of human nature, self-love belongs also to one's rational nature—it "belongs to man as a reasonable creature reflecting on his own
interest or happiness." Thus, self-love is a kind of second-
order desire; it can acquire a particular object (prompt us to
perform some particular action) only after we have deliberated
concerning the objects of our particular first-order desires
and determined their bearing on (by way of promoting or hinder-
ing) our own good or happiness.

(2) Butler later draws an important consequence from this
observation. If self-love is a general desire for our own happiness, and if "happiness or satisfaction consists only in the
enjoyment of those objects which are by nature suited to our
several particular appetites, passions, and affections" (as,
e.g., eating food is suited to hunger), then our particular desires must be logically prior to self-love, since if we had no
particular desires, there would be nothing to constitute our
happiness, and thus self-love would have no object. Thus, it
is absurd to suppose that all our motives could somehow be reduced to that of self-love. For if this were possible, it
would also be possible for self-love to be our one and only
motive. But this we have seen to be (conceptually) impossible.

(3) Confusion is also apt to arise from failure to observe that the objects of our particular desires are "*external
things themselves*, distinct from the *pleasure arising from
them*." That this is so can be seen, says Butler, if we note
that had we no desire for such external objects, we should derive no pleasure from obtaining them. As Butler points out, if
a man did not desire food, he would derive no more pleasure
from eating food than from swallowing a stone. Thus, one does
not desire to eat food *because* he desires the pleasure of eat-

ing food; rather, he derives pleasure from eating food only because he desires to eat food.

It has been suggested that Butler somewhat overstates his
case at this point. As C. D. Broad points out, "We must distinguish between those pleasures which consist in the fulfill-
ment of pre-existing desires and those which do not":

> Certain sensations are intrinsically pleasant,
> e.g., the smell of violets or the taste of sugar.
> Others are intrinsically unpleasant, e.g., the smell
> of sulphurated hydrogen or the feel of a burn. We
> must therefore distinguish between intrinsic pleasures
> and pains and the pleasures and pains of satisfied or
> frustrated impulse.[16]

These two kinds of pleasure are distinct, even though, as Broad
points out, they may at times coincide—e.g., when "I am hungry
and eat some specially nice food," "I have then both the intrin-
sically pleasant sensations of taste and also the pleasure of
satisfying my hunger." It is obvious that Butler's observation
is true only of the pleasures of satisfied impulse and not of
intrinsic pleasures. For, to use Broad's example, "A *bon vi-
vant* towards the end of a long dinner might get an intrinsical-
ly pleasant sensation of taste from his savoury although he was
no longer hungry and therefore did not get the pleasures of
satisfying his hunger."[17] However, this restriction of Butler's remarks to those pleasures which consist simply in the
gratification of one's desires does nothing to mar his argument,
for it is on those pleasures, and not on the intrinsic pleasures, that the psychological egoist rests his case.

(4) Nor can the hedonistic psychological egoist appeal
for support to the fact that the pleasure arising from the
gratification of any particular desire is always *one's own
pleasure*. If this is one's ground for asserting that all actions are egoistic, self-interested, or motivated by self-love,
then one has purchased evidence for one's thesis at the cost of
trivializing it. For if the psychological egoist's hypothesis
is to be a significant empirical hypothesis, then it must at
least be *logically possible* for actions which are not egoistic,
self-interested, or motivated by self-love to exist (even if,
as the psychological egoist contends, such actions are *psychologically impossible* and thus never occur). But if the psychological egoist bases his thesis on (a) whenever a person
acts voluntarily, he does what he, in some sense, desires

---

[16]Broad, *Five Types of Ethical Theory*, p. 66.

[17]Ibid., p. 67.

(wants) to do, and (b) whenever a person does what he desires
to do, he derives a pleasure from the gratification of that desire, then he does make nonegoistic actions logically impossible. As Butler puts it, "According to this way of speaking,
no creature whatever can *possibly* act but merely from self-
love" (italics are mine). For if (a) is true, it is true only
in a trivial sense that makes it logically impossible for anyone to voluntarily do that which he does not desire (want) to
do. Ordinarily, we do speak of people as sometimes voluntarily
doing that which they do not really want to do. Consider Aristotle's famous example of the captain who jettisons some of
his cargo in order to save his ship. He chooses to jettison
the cargo and thus acts voluntarily, since he prefers to save
the ship rather than lose both the cargo and the ship. Does he
really want to jettison the cargo? If we answer yes, this can
only be because we are prepared to say this whenever a person
does what he chooses or prefers to do. In short, we are prepared to say that (a) is true merely in virtue of the definition of a voluntary action.

 Moreover, (b) will support the egoist's conclusion only if
the pleasure derived from the gratification of one's desire is
supposed also to be the object of one's desire. For only then
will it follow that whenever a person acts voluntarily, he acts
for the sake of some pleasure for himself, and thus (to use
Hobbes's phrase) for the sake of "some good to himself." But
we have already noted the mistake involved in confusing the object of a particular desire with that pleasure arising merely
from its gratification.

 (5) Again, we have already noted the absurdity involved
in failing to distinguish self-love from the particular desires
(appetites, passions, and affections) and of attempting to reduce all desires to that of self-love. Thus, even the trivial
sense in which it may be true to say that whenever a person
acts voluntarily, he does what he desires to do will not support the egoist's claim that all actions are motivated by self-
love. Furthermore, not only are the particular desires distinct from self-love, they may conflict with it:

> For nothing is more common than to see men give them-
> selves up to a passion or an affection to their known
> prejudice and ruin, and in direct contradiction to
> manifest and real interest, and the loudest calls of
> self-love. . . .[18]

Shall one insist that even here, since one does what one desires to do, one is motivated by self-love?

---

[18]See p. 34 of this volume.

(6) Finally, Butler turns to the relationship between self-love and benevolence. Benevolence ("an affection to the good of our fellow-creatures") bears the same relationship to self-love as do the particular desires from which self-love has been distinguished. Thus, benevolence is no more incompatible with self-love than are such particular desires as hunger, envy, and lust. Indeed, Butler believes it to be more compatible with self-love than many of these desires, since, for many of us, the enjoyments we derive from helping others are among the principal ingredients of our happiness.

The belief that there is some special incompatibility between benevolence and self-love arises from confusing the two quite distinct ideas of self-love and selfishness. One who loves his neighbor will be "gratified by a consciousness of endeavoring to promote the good of others." And the gratification of this affection has just the same relationship to our interests and to self-love as does the gratification of any other affection. Insofar as I do have this affection, its gratification will be one of the ingredients of my happiness, and promoting the good of others will thus be for me an end of self-love. Thus, there is no necessary incompatibility between self-love and love for our neighbors. Selfishness is quite different, however, for we call an action selfish just insofar as one has disregarded the effects of his action on the interests or good of others.

The selection from Schlick represents still another attempt to understand what might be meant in calling actions and motives egoistic. Schlick agrees with Butler that "the satisfaction of an impulse is never in itself egoistic." Nor can selfishness (egoism as a state of character) be characterized as consisting in actions done from some peculiar "egoistic" motive. No such motive (or even set of motives), universally determining all conduct, is to be found. It is rather the satisfaction of an impulse in utter disregard of the interests of others (inconsideration) that constitutes selfishness.

The selections from Broad and Slote represent attempts to formulate the thesis of psychological egoism in such a way as to avoid the kinds of conceptual confusion pointed out by Butler. Accepting Butler's major observations as sound, Broad argues that only a pluralistic version of psychological egoism could possibly "fit the facts of human life." Such a view holds that although there is more than one ultimate motive of actions, all of the ultimate motives of action are in some sense "egoistic." Broad attempts to explicate the meaning of the term 'egoistic' so employed in terms of such criteria as "self-confined," "self-centered," and "other-regarding but self-referential," each of which he defines in turn. He then invites us to consider the plausibility of psychological egoism so defined. Slote sees psychological egoism as entailed by a

scientific hypothesis (suggested by some behavioristic learning theorists) that is subject to both empirical refutation and
confirmation.

ALTRUISM, BENEVOLENCE, AND SYMPATHY

The readings from Hume, Kant, Justin Aronfreed, and Thomas
Nagel have been selected because of the contributions they make
toward clarifying such concepts as benevolence, sympathy, and
altruism. Hume and Kant present contrasting conceptions of
benevolence and of the relationship between benevolence and
self-love. Hume argues that the possibility of making moral
judgments presupposes a peculiar sentiment (that of benevolence, humanity, or sympathy) distinct from and not reducible
to self-love or self-interest. Such a sentiment also does exist, because human beings are such that the contemplation of
the happiness or misery of others just in and of itself "excites in our breast a sympathetic movement of pleasure or uneasiness." Thus, altruism and benevolence are constituted by
a capacity, which all men have in at least some measure, to
be directly moved by the happiness or misery of others—"the
view of the former . . . communicates a secret joy and satisfaction; the appearance of the latter . . . throws a melancholy
damp over the imagination."
The importance of Kant lies in the fact that he proposes a
conception of benevolence (and altruism), based on the distinction between pathological love and practical love, that is radically different from the account proposed by Hume, and also in
the fact that, unlike Hume, he proposes a theory of rational
motivation which (as we have already pointed out) is wholly at
odds with the presuppositions of psychological egoism. For
Kant, practical benevolence consists in doing good to others
from duty "rather than from inclination (love) toward others."
Indeed, "to help other men according to our ability is a duty,
whether we love them or not." Practical love, as opposed to
love as a feeling (pathological or emotional love), consists in
the disposition to exercise such a duty. For Kant, genuine altruism must be sharply distinguished from a disposition to action arising out of sympathy ("sensuous feelings of pleasure or
pain . . . at another's state of happiness or sadness"). The
virtuous man will make use of such feelings (if he happens to
have them) "as means to promoting active and rational benevolence," but genuine altruism requires no such stimulus.
Thus, if Kant is right, James Boswell's attribution of the
following statement to Samuel Johnson does represent a genuine
psychological possibility: "I own, Sir, I have not so much
feeling for the distress of others as some people have or pretend to have; but I know this, that I would do all in my power

to relieve them."[19]   And, as F. C. Sharp has pointed out: "In persons without altruism, sympathy—like love—will not produce acts of genuine altruism but, where sympathy is painful, only an attempt to get rid of the reflected suffering by the shortest way practicable."[20]   Sharp cites the example of "the man who always rode in the street car with his eyes closed, because he could not bear to see ladies standing when he had a seat."[21]

The selections from Aronfreed and Nagel represent contrasting conceptions of altruism that parallel in important respects the contrasts between Hume and Kant.   Aronfreed proposes a conception of altruism that makes altruistic behavior a function of the agent's capacity for empathic or vicarious experience. Nagel, on the other hand, insists that there is a kind of altruism that can be explained neither in terms of self-interest nor in terms of such general sentiments as benevolence or sympathy. Pure altruism, he suggests, is a rational requirement on action, consisting of "the direct influence of one person's interest on the actions of another, simply because in itself the interest of the former provides the latter with a reason to act."

Thomas Hobbes

SELF-LOVE AND SOCIETY

From *Philosophical Rudiments Concerning Government and Society (De Cive)*, 1642.   Reprinted here is chapter 1, "Of the State of Men without Society," from the Molesworth edition of 1841.   Thomas Hobbes (1588–1679), who became notorious for his so-called selfish hypothesis, is also important for his contributions to the social-contract theory of government.   Besides the work from which this selection is taken, he also defends egoism (both psychological and ethical) in *The Elements of Law (De Corpore Politico)* and *Leviathan*.

[19]James Boswell, *Life of Samuel Johnson*, vol. 2. (Hill Edition), p. 537.   Quoted by F. C. Sharp, *Ethics* (New York and London: Century Co., 1928), p. 494.

[20]Sharp, *Ethics*, p. 494.

[21]Ibid., p. 76.

1. The faculties of human nature may be reduced unto four
kinds; bodily strength, experience, reason, passion. Taking
the beginning of this following doctrine from these, we will
declare, in the first place, what manner of inclinations men
who are endued with these faculties bear towards each other,
and whether, and by what faculty they are born apt for society,
and to preserve themselves against mutual violence; then proceeding, we will shew what advice was necessary to be taken for
this business, and what are the conditions of society, or of
human peace; that is to say, (changing the words only), what
are the fundamental *laws of nature*.

2. The greatest part of those men who have written aught
concerning commonwealths, either suppose, or require us or beg
of us to believe, that man is a creature born fit[1] for society.
The Greeks call him ζωον πολιτικον; and on this foundation they
so build up the doctrine of civil society, as if for the preservation of peace, and the government of mankind, there were

---

[1]*Born fit.*] Since we now see actually a constituted society
among men, and none living out of it, since we discern all desirous of congress and mutual correspondence, it may seem a
wonderful kind of stupidity, to lay in the very threshold of
this doctrine such a stumbling block before the reader, as to
deny *man to be born fit for society*. Therefore I must more
plainly say, that it is true indeed, that to man by nature, or
as man, that is, as soon as he is born, solitude is an enemy;
for infants have need of others to help them to live, and those
of riper years to help them to live well. Wherefore I deny not
that men (even nature compelling) desire to come together. But
civil societies are not mere meetings, but bonds, to the making
whereof faith and compacts are necessary; the virtue whereof to
children and fools, and the profit whereof to those who have
not yet tasted the miseries which accompany its defects, is altogether unknown; whence it happens, that those, because they
know not what society is, cannot enter into it; these, because
ignorant of the benefit it brings, care not for it. Manifest
therefore it is, that all men, because they are born in infan-
cy, are born unapt for society. Many also, perhaps most men,
either through defect of mind or want of education, remain unfit during the whole course of their lives; yet have they, infants as well as those of riper years, a human nature. Wherefore man is made fit for society not by nature, but by education. Furthermore, although man were born in such a condition
as to desire it, it follows not, that he therefore were born
fit to enter into it. For it is one thing to desire, another
to be in capacity fit for what we desire; for even they, who
through their pride, will not stoop to equal conditions, without which there can be no society, do yet desire it.

nothing else necessary than that men should agree to make certain covenants and conditions together, which themselves should then call laws. Which axiom, though received by most, is yet certainly false; and an error proceeding from our too slight contemplation of human nature. For they who shall more narrowly look into the causes for which men come together, and delight in each other's company, shall easily find that this happens not because naturally it could happen no otherwise, but by accident. For if by nature one man should love another, that is, as man, there could no reason be returned why every man should not equally love every man, as being equally man; or why he should rather frequent those, whose society affords him honour or profit. We do not therefore by nature seek society for its own sake, but that we may receive some honour or profit from it; these we desire primarily, that secondarily. How, by what advice, men do meet, will be best known by observing those things which they do when they are met. For if they meet for traffic, it is plain every man regards not his fellow, but his business; if to discharge some office, a certain market-friendship is begotten, which hath more of jealousy in it than true love, and whence factions sometimes may arise, but good will never; if for pleasure and recreation of mind, every man is wont to please himself most with those things which stir up laughter, whence he may, according to the nature of that which is ridiculous, by comparison of another man's defects and infirmities, pass the more current in his own opinion. And although this be sometimes innocent and without offence, yet it is manifest they are not so much delighted with the society, as their own vain glory. But for the most part, in these kinds of meeting we wound the absent; their whole life, sayings, actions are examined, judged, condemned. Nay, it is very rare but some present receive a fling as soon as they part; so as his reason was not ill, who was wont always at parting to go out last. And these are indeed the true delights of society, unto which we are carried by nature, that is, by those passions which are incident to all creatures, until either by sad experience or good precepts it so fall out, which in many it never happens, that the appetite of present matters be dulled with the memory of things past: without which the discourse of most quick and nimble men on this subject, is but cold and hungry.
  But if it so happen, that being met they pass their time in relating some stories, and one of them begins to tell one which concerns himself; instantly every one of the rest most greedily desires to speak of himself too; if one relate some wonder, the rest will tell you miracles, if they have them; if not, they will feign them. Lastly, that I may say somewhat of them who pretend to be wiser than others: if they meet to talk of philosophy, look, how many men, so many would be esteemed masters, or else they not only love not their fellows, but even

persecute them with hatred. So clear is it by experience to
all men who a little more narrowly consider human affairs,
that all free congress ariseth either from mutual poverty, or
from vain glory, whence the parties met endeavour to carry with
them either some benefit, or to leave behind them that same
ἐυδοκιμεῖν, some esteem and honour with those, with whom they
have been conversant. The same is also collected by reason out
of the definitions themselves of *will, good, honour, profitable*.
For when we voluntarily contract society, in all manner of society we look after the object of the will, that is, that which
every one of those who gather together, propounds to himself
for good. Now whatsoever seems good, is pleasant, and relates
either to the senses, or the mind. But all the mind's pleasure
is either glory, (or to have a good opinion of one's self), or
refers to glory in the end; the rest are sensual, or conducing
to sensuality, which may be all comprehended under the word
conveniences. All society therefore is either for gain, or for
glory; that is, not so much for love of our fellows, as for the
love of ourselves. But no society can be great or lasting,
which begins from vain glory. Because that glory is like honour; if all men have it no man hath it, for they consist in
comparison and precedence. Neither doth the society of others
advance any whit the cause of my glorying in myself; for every
man must account himself, such as he can make himself without
the help of others. But though the benefits of this life may
be much furthered by mutual help, since yet those may be better
attained to by dominion than by the society of others, I hope
no body will doubt, but that men would much more greedily be
carried by nature, if all fear were removed, to obtain dominion,
than to gain society. We must therefore resolve, that the
original of all great and lasting societies consisted not in
the mutual good will men had towards each other, but in the mutual fear[2] they had of each other.

---

[2]*The mutual fear.*] It is objected: it is so improbable that
men should grow into civil societies out of fear, that if they
had been afraid, they would not have endured each other's looks.
They presume, I believe, that to fear is nothing else than to
be affrighted. I comprehend in this word *fear*, a certain fore-
sight of future evil; neither do I conceive flight the sole
property of fear, but to distrust, suspect, take heed, provide
so that they may not fear, is also incident to the fearful.
They who go to sleep, shut their doors; they who travel, carry
their swords with them, because they fear thieves. Kingdoms
guard their coasts and frontiers with forts and castles; cities
are compact with walls; and all for fear of neighbouring kingdoms and towns. Even the strongest armies, and most accomplished for fight, yet sometimes parley for peace, as fearing
each other's power, and lest they might be overcome. It is

3. The cause of mutual fear consists partly in the natural equality of men, partly in their mutual will of hurting: whence it comes to pass, that we can neither expect from others, nor promise to ourselves the least security. For if we look on men full-grown, and consider how brittle the frame of our human body is, which perishing, all its strength, vigour, and wisdom itself perisheth with it; and how easy a matter it is, even for the weakest man to kill the strongest: there is no reason why any man, trusting to his own strength, should conceive himself made by nature above others. They are equals, who can do equal things one against the other; but they who can do the greatest things, namely, kill, can do equal things. All men therefore among themselves are by nature equal; the inequality we now discern, hath its spring from the civil law.

4. All men in the state of nature have a desire and will to hurt, but not proceeding from the same cause, neither equally to be condemned. For one man, according to that natural equality which is among us, permits as much to others as he assumes himself; which is an argument of a temperate man, and one that rightly values his power. Another, supposing himself above others, will have a license to do what he lists, and challenges respect and honour, as due to him before others; which is an argument of a fiery spirit. This man's will to hurt ariseth from vain glory, and the false esteem he hath of his own strength; the other's from the necessity of defending himself, his liberty, and his goods, against this man's violence.

5. Furthermore, since the combat of wits is the fiercest, the greatest discords which are, must necessarily arise from this contention. For in this case it is not only odious to contend against, but also not to consent. For not to approve of what a man saith, is no less than tacitly to accuse him of an error in that thing which he speaketh: as in very many things to dissent, is as much as if you accounted him a fool whom you dissent from. Which may appear hence, that there are no wars so sharply waged as between sects of the same religion, and factions of the same commonweal, where the contestation is either concerning doctrines or politic prudence. And since all the pleasure and jollity of the mind consists in this, even to get some, with whom comparing, it may find somewhat wherein to triumph and vaunt itself; it is impossible but men must declare

---

[2](cont.) through fear that men secure themselves by flight indeed, and in corners, if they think they cannot escape otherwise; but for the most part, by arms and defensive weapons; whence it happens, that daring to come forth they know each other's spirits. But then if they fight, civil society ariseth from the victory; if they agree, from their agreement.

sometimes some mutual scorn and contempt, either by laughter, or by words, or by gesture, or some sign or other; than which there is no greater vexation of mind, and than from which there cannot possibly arise a greater desire to do hurt.

6. But the most frequent reason why men desire to hurt each other, ariseth hence, that many men at the same time have an appetite to the same thing; which yet very often they can neither enjoy in common, nor yet divide it; whence it follows that the strongest must have it, and who is strongest must be decided by the sword.

7. Among so many dangers therefore, as the natural lusts of men do daily threaten each other withal, to have a care of one's self is so far from being a matter scornfully to be looked upon, that one has neither the power nor wish to have done otherwise. For every man is desirous of what is good for him, and shuns what is evil, but chiefly the chiefest of natural evils, which is death; and this he doth by a certain impulsion of nature, no less than that whereby a stone moves downward. It is therefore neither absurd nor reprehensible, neither against the dictates of true reason, for a man to use all his endeavours to preserve and defend his body and the members thereof from death and sorrows. But that which is not contrary to right reason, that all men account to be done justly, and with right. Neither by the word *right* is anything else signified, than that liberty which every man hath to make use of his natural faculties according to right reason. Therefore the first foundation of natural right is this, that *every man as much as in him lies endeavour to protect his life and members*.

8. But because it is in vain for a man to have a right to the end, if the right to the necessary means be denied him, it follows, that since every man hath a right to preserve himself, he must also be allowed a right *to use all the means, and do all the actions, without which he cannot preserve himself.*

9. Now whether the means which he is about to use, and the action he is performing, be necessary to the preservation of his life and members or not, he himself, by the right of nature, must be judge. For if it be contrary to right reason that I should judge of mine own peril, say, that another man is judge. Why now, because he judgeth of what concerns me, by the same reason, because we are equal by nature, will I judge also of things which do belong to him? Therefore it agrees with right reason, that is, it is the right of nature that I judge of his opinion, that is, whether it conduce to my preservation or not.

10. Nature hath given to *every one a right to all*; that is, it was lawful for every man, in the bare state of nature,[3] or before such time as men had engaged themselves by any covenants or bonds, to do what he would, and against whom he thought fit, and to possess, use, and enjoy all that he would, or could get. Now because whatsoever a man would, it therefore seems good to him because he wills it, and either it really doth, or at least seems to him to contribute towards his preservation, (but we have already allowed him to be judge, in the foregoing article, whether it doth or not, insomuch as we are to hold all for necessary whatsoever he shall esteem so), and by the 7th article it appears that by the right of nature those things may be done, and must be had, which necessarily conduce to the protection of life and members, it follows, that in the state of nature, to have all, and do all, is lawful for all. And this is that which is meant by that common saying, *nature*

---

[3]*In the bare state of nature.*] This is thus to be understood: what any man does in the bare state of nature, is injurious to no man; not that in such a state he cannot offend God, or break the laws of nature; for injustice against men presupposeth human laws, such as in the state of nature there are none. Now the truth of this proposition thus conceived, is sufficiently demonstrated to the mindful reader in the articles immediately foregoing; but because in certain cases the difficulty of the conclusion makes us forget the premises, I will contract this argument, and make it most evident to a single view. Every man hath right to protect himself, as appears by the seventh article. The same man therefore hath a right to use all the means which necessarily conduce to this end, by the eighth article. But those are the necessary means which he shall judge to be such, by the ninth article. He therefore hath a right to make use of, and to do all whatsoever he shall judge requisite for his preservation; wherefore by the judgment of him that doth it, the thing done is either right or wrong, and therefore right. True it is therefore in the bare state of nature, &c. But if any man pretend somewhat to tend necessarily to his preservation, which yet he himself doth not confidently believe so, he may offend against the laws of nature, as in the third chapter of this book is more at large declared. It hath been objected by some: if a son kill his father, doth he him no injury? I have answered, that a son cannot be understood to be at any time in the state of nature, as being under the power and command of them to whom he owes his protection as soon as ever he is born, namely, either his father's or his mother's, or him that nourished him; as is demonstrated in the ninth chapter.

hath given all to all. From whence we understand likewise, that in the state of nature profit is the measure of right.

11.   But it was the least benefit for men thus to have a common right to all things. For the effects of this right are the same, almost, as if there had been no right at all. For although any man might say of every thing, *this is mine*, yet could he not enjoy it, by reason of his neighbour, who having equal right and equal power, would pretend the same thing to be his.

12.   If now to this natural proclivity of men, to hurt each other, which they derive from their passions, but chiefly from a vain esteem of themselves, you add, the right of all to all, wherewith one by right invades, the other by right resists, and whence arise perpetual jealousies and suspicions on all hands, and how hard a thing it is to provide against an enemy invading us with an intention to oppress and ruin, though he come with a small number, and no great provision; it cannot be denied but that the natural state of men, before they entered into society, was a mere war, and that not simply, but a war of all men against all men. For what is WAR, but that same time in which the will of contesting by force is fully declared, either by words or deeds? The time remaining is termed PEACE.

13.   But it is easily judged how disagreeable a thing to the preservation either of mankind, or of each single man, a perpetual war is. But it is perpetual in its own nature; because in regard of the equality of those that strive, it cannot be ended by victory. For in this state the conqueror is subject to so much danger, as it were to be accounted a miracle, if any, even the most strong, should close up his life with many years and old age. They of America are examples hereof, even in this present age: other nations have been in former ages; which now indeed are become civil and flourishing, but were then few, fierce, short-lived, poor, nasty, and deprived of all that pleasure and beauty of life, which peace and society are wont to bring with them. Whosoever therefore holds, that it had been best to have continued in that state in which all things were lawful for all men, he contradicts himself. For every man by natural necessity desires that which is good for him: nor is there any that esteems a war of all against all, which necessarily adheres to such a state, to be good for him. And so it happens, that through fear of each other we think it fit to rid ourselves of this condition, and to get some fellows; that if there needs must be war, it may not yet be against all men, nor without some helps.

14.   Fellows are gotten either by constraint, or by consent; by constraint, when after fight the conqueror makes the conquered serve him, either through fear of death, or by laying fetters on him: by consent, when men enter into society to help each other, both parties consenting without any constraint.

But the conqueror may by right compel the conquered, or the strongest the weaker, (as a man in health may one that is sick, or he that is of riper years a child), unless he will choose to die, to give caution of his future obedience. For since the right of protecting ourselves according to our own wills, proceeded from our danger, and our danger from our equality, it is more consonant to reason, and more certain for our conservation, using the present advantage to secure ourselves by taking caution, than when they shall be full grown and strong, and got out of our power, to endeavour to recover that power again by doubtful fight. And on the other side, nothing can be thought more absurd, than by discharging whom you already have weak in your power, to make him at once both an enemy and a strong one. From whence we may understand likewise as a corollary in the natural state of men, that *a sure and irresistible power confers the right of dominion and ruling over those who cannot resist*; insomuch, as the right of all things that can be done, adheres essentially and immediately unto this omnipotence hence arising.

15. Yet cannot men expect any lasting preservation, continuing thus in the state of nature, that is, of war, by reason of that equality of power, and other human faculties they are endued withal. Wherefore to seek peace, where there is any hopes of obtaining it, and where there is none, to enquire out for auxiliaries of war, is the dictate of right reason, that is, the law of nature. . . .

Joseph Butler

UPON THE LOVE OF OUR NEIGHBOUR

From *Fifteen Sermons upon Human Nature* (London, 1726), 2d ed., 1729. Reprinted here is Sermon 11. Joseph Butler (1692–1752) is considered by many to have provided a decisive refutation of psychological egoism. As C. D. Broad so amusingly puts it: "As a psychological theory it was killed by Butler; but it still flourishes, I believe, among bookmakers and smart young business men whose claim to know the world is based on an intimate acquaintance with the shadier side of it. In Butler's day the theory moved in higher social and intellectual circles, and it had to

be treated more seriously than any philosopher would
trouble to treat it now. This change is very largely
the result of Butler's work; he killed the theory so
thoroughly that he sometimes seems to the modern reader to be flogging dead horses. Still, all good fallacies go to America when they die, and rise again as
the latest discoveries of the local professors. So
it will always be useful to have Butler's refutation
at hand." (*Five Types of Ethical Theory*, p. 55.)

And if there be any other commandment, it is
briefly comprehended in this saying, namely, Thou
shalt love thy neighbour as thyself.—Rom. xiii. 9.

It is commonly observed, that there is a disposition in
men to complain of the viciousness and corruption of the age in
which they live, as greater than that of former ones; which is
usually followed with this further observation, that mankind
has been in that respect much the same in all times. Now, not
to determine whether this last be not contradicted by the accounts of history; thus much can scarce be doubted, that vice
and folly takes different turns, and some particular kinds of
it are more open and avowed in some ages than in others: and,
I suppose, it may be spoken of as very much the distinction of
the present to profess a contracted spirit, and greater regards
to self-interest, than appears to have been done formerly. Upon this account it seems worth while to inquire whether private
interest is likely to be promoted in proportion to the degree
in which self-love engrosses us, and prevails over all other
principles; or *whether the contracted affection may not possibly be so prevalent as to disappoint itself, and even contradict its own end, private good.*
And since further, there is generally thought to be some
peculiar kind of contrariety between self-love and the love of
our neighbour, between the pursuit of public and of private
good; insomuch that when you are recommending one of these, you
are supposed to be speaking against the other; and from hence
arises a secret prejudice against, and frequently open scorn
of, all talk of public spirit, and real good-will to our fellow-
creatures; it will be necessary to *inquire what respect benevolence hath to self-love, and the pursuit of private interest to
the pursuit of public*: or whether there be anything of that peculiar inconsistence and contrariety between them, over and
above what there is between self-love and other passions and
particular affections, and their respective pursuits.
These inquiries, it is hoped, may be favourably attended
to: for there shall be all possible concessions made to the
favourite passion, which hath so much allowed to it, and whose
cause is so universally pleaded: it shall be treated with the
utmost tenderness and concern for its interests.

In order to do this, as well as to determine the forementioned questions, it will be necessary to *consider the nature, the object and end of that self-love, as distinguished from other principles or affections in the mind, and their respective objects.*

Every man hath a general desire of his own happiness; and likewise a variety of particular affections, passions and appetites to particular external objects. The former proceeds from, or is self-love; and seems inseparable from all sensible creatures, who can reflect upon themselves and their own interest or happiness, so as to have that interest an object to their minds: what is to be said of the latter is, that they proceed from, or together make up that particular nature, according to which man is made. The object the former pursues is somewhat internal, our own happiness, enjoyment, satisfaction; whether we have, or have not, a distinct particular perception what it is, or wherein it consists: the objects of the latter are this or that particular external thing, which the affections tend towards, and of which it hath always a particular idea or perception. The principle we call self-love never seeks anything external for the sake of the thing, but only as a means of happiness or good: particular affections rest in the external things themselves. One belongs to man as a reasonable creature reflecting upon his own interest or happiness. The others, though quite distinct from reason, are as much a part of human nature.

That all particular appetites and passions are towards *external things themselves,* distinct from the *pleasure arising from them,* is manifested from hence; that there could not be this pleasure, were it not for that prior suitableness between the object and the passion: there could be no enjoyment or delight from one thing more than another, from eating food more than from swallowing a stone, if there were not an affection or appetite to one thing more than another.

Every particular affection, even the love of our neighbour, is as really our own affection, as self-love; and the pleasure arising from its gratification is as much my own pleasure, as the pleasure self-love would have, from knowing I myself should be happy some time hence, would be my own pleasure. And if, because every particular affection is a man's own, and the pleasure arising from its gratification his own pleasure, or pleasure to himself, such particular affection must be called self-love; according to this way of speaking, no creature whatever can possibly act but merely from self-love; and every action and every affection whatever is to be resolved up into this one principle. But, then, this is not the language of mankind: or if it were, we should want words to express the difference between the principle of an action, proceeding from cool consideration that it will be to my own advantage; and an

action, suppose of revenge, or of friendship, by which a man
runs upon certain ruin, to do evil or good to another. It is
manifest the principles of these actions are totally different,
and so want different words to be distinguished by: all that
they agree in is, that they both proceed from, and are done to
gratify, an inclination in a man's self. But the principle or
inclination in one case is self-love: in the other, hatred or
love of another. There is then a distinction between the cool
principle of self-love, or general desire of our own happiness,
as one part of our nature, and one principle of action; and the
particular affections towards particular external objects, as
another part of our nature, and another principle of action.
How much soever therefore is to be allowed to self-love, yet it
cannot be allowed to be the whole of our inward constitution;
because, you see, there are other parts or principles which
come into it.

Further, private happiness or good is all which self-love
can make us desire, or be concerned about: in having this consists its gratification; it is an affection to ourselves; it is a
regard to our own interest, happiness and private good: and in
the proportion a man hath this, he is interested, or a lover of
himself. Let this be kept in mind; because there is commonly,
as I shall presently have occasion to observe, another sense
put upon these words. On the other hand, particular affections
tend towards particular external things: these are their objects; having these is their end: in this consists their gratification: no matter whether it be, or be not, upon the whole,
our interest or happiness. An action done from the former of
these principles is called an interested action. An action
proceeding from any of the latter has its denomination of pas-
sionate, ambitious, friendly, revengeful, or any other, from
the particular appetite or affection from which it proceeds.
Thus self-love as one part of human nature, and the several
particular principles as the other part, are, themselves, their
objects and ends, stated and shewn.

From hence it will be easy to see, how far, and in what
ways, each of these can contribute and be subservient to the
private good of the individual. Happiness does not consist in
self-love. The desire of happiness is no more the thing itself,
than the desire of riches is the possession or enjoyment of
them. People may love themselves with the most entire and unbounded affection, and yet be extremely miserable. Neither can
self-love any way help them out, but by setting them on work to
get rid of the causes of their misery, to gain or make use of
those objects which are by nature adapted to afford satisfaction. Happiness or satisfaction consists only in the enjoyment
of those objects, which are by nature suited to our several
particular appetites, passions and affections. So that if self-
love wholly engrosses us, and leaves no room for any other

principle, there can be absolutely no such thing at all as happiness, or enjoyment of any kind whatever; since happiness consists in the gratification of particular passions, which supposes the having of them. Self-love, then, does not constitute *this* or *that* to be our interest or good; but, our interest or good being constituted by nature and supposed, self-love only puts us upon obtaining and securing it. Therefore, if it be possible, that self-love may prevail and exert itself in a degree or manner which is not subservient to this end; then it will not follow, that our interest will be promoted in proportion to the degree in which that principle engrosses us, and prevails over others. Nay further, the private and contracted affection, when it is not subservient to this end, private good, may, for anything that appears, have a direct contrary tendency and effect. And if we will consider the matter, we shall see that it often really has. *Disengagement* is absolutely necessary to enjoyment: and a person may have so steady and fixed an eye upon his own interest, whatever he places it in, as may hinder him from *attending* to many gratifications within his reach, which others have their minds *free* and *open* to. Overfondness for a child is not generally thought to be for its advantage: and, if there be any guess to be made from appearances, surely that character we call selfish is not the most promising for happiness. Such a temper may plainly be and exert itself in a degree and manner which may give unnecessary and useless solicitude and anxiety, in a degree and manner which may prevent obtaining the means and materials of enjoyment, as well as the making use of them. Immoderate self-love does very ill consult its own interest: and, how much soever a paradox it may appear, it is certainly true, that even from self-love we should endeavour to get over all inordinate regard to, and consideration of ourselves. Everyone of our passions and affections hath its natural stint and bound, which may easily be exceeded; whereas our enjoyments can possibly be but in a determinate measure and degree. Therefore such excess of the affection, since it cannot procure any enjoyment, must in all cases be useless; but is generally attended with inconveniences, and often is downright pain and misery. This holds as much with regard to self-love as to all other affections. The natural degree of it, so far as it sets us on work to gain and make use of the materials of satisfaction, may be to our real advantage; but beyond or besides this, it is in several respects an inconvenience and disadvantage. Thus it appears, that private interest is so far from being likely to be promoted in proportion to the degree in which self-love engrosses us, and prevails over all other principles; that *the contracted affection may be so prevalent as to disappoint itself, and even contradict its own end, private good.*

"But who, except the most sordidly covetous, ever thought there was any rivalship between the love of greatness, honour, power, or between sensual appetites, and self-love? No, there is a perfect harmony between them. It is by means of these particular appetites and affections that self-love is gratified in enjoyment, happiness and satisfaction. The competition and rivalship is between self-love and the love of our neighbour: that affection which leads us out of ourselves, makes us regardless of our own interest, and substitute that of another in its stead." Whether then there be any peculiar competition and contrariety in this case, shall now be considered.

Self-love and interestedness was stated to consist in or be an affection to ourselves, a regard to our own private good: it is therefore distinct from benevolence, which is an affection to the good of our fellow-creatures. But that benevolence is distinct from, that is, not the same thing with self-love, is no reason for its being looked upon with any peculiar suspicion; because every principle whatever, by means of which self-love is gratified, is distinct from it: and all things which are distinct from each other are equally so. A man has an affection or aversion to another: that one of these tends to and is gratified by doing good, that the other tends to and is gratified by doing harm, does not in the least alter the respect which either one or the other of these inward feelings has to self-love. We use the word *property* so as to exclude any other persons having an interest in that of which we say a particular man has the property. And we often use the word *selfish* so as to exclude in the same manner all regards to the good of others. But the cases are not parallel: for though that exclusion is really part of the idea of property; yet such positive exclusion, or bringing this peculiar disregard to the good of others into the idea of self-love, is in reality adding to the idea, or changing it from what it was before stated to consist in, namely, in an affection to ourselves. This being the whole idea of self-love, it can no otherwise exclude goodwill or love of others, than merely by not including it, nor otherwise, than it excludes love of arts or of reputation, or of anything else. Neither on the other hand does benevolence, any more than love of arts or reputation, exclude self-love. Love of our neighbour then has just the same respect to, is no more distant from self-love, than hatred of our neighbour, or than love or hatred of anything else. Thus the principles, from which men rush upon certain ruin for the destruction of an enemy, and for the preservation of a friend, have the same respect to the private affection, and are equally interested, or equally disinterested: and it is of no avail, whether they are said to be one or the other. Therefore to those who are shocked to hear virtue spoken of as disinterested, it may be allowed that it is indeed absurd to speak thus of it; unless

hatred, several particular instances of vice, and all the common affections and aversions in mankind, are acknowledged to be
disinterested too. Is there any less inconsistence between the
love of inanimate things, or of creatures merely sensitive, and
self-love; than between self-love and the love of our neighbour?
Is desire of and delight in the happiness of another any more a
diminution of self-love, than desire of and delight in the esteem of another? They are both equally desire of and delight
in somewhat external to ourselves: either both or neither are
so. The object of self-love is expressed in the term self; and
every appetite of sense, and every particular affection of the
heart, are equally interested or disinterested, because the objects of them all are equally self or somewhat else. Whatever
ridicule therefore the mention of a disinterested principle or
action may be supposed to lie open to, must, upon the matter
thus stated, relate to ambition, and every appetite and particular affection, as much as to benevolence. And indeed all the
ridicule, and all the grave perplexity, of which this subject
hath had its full share, is merely from words. The most intelligible way of speaking of it seems to be this: that self-love,
and the actions done in consequence of it (for these will
presently appear to be the same as to this question) are interested; that particular affections towards external objects, and
the actions done in consequence of those affections, are not so.
But every one is at liberty to use words as he pleases. All
that is here insisted upon is, that ambition, revenge, benevolence, all particular passions whatever, and the actions they
produce, are equally interested or disinterested.

Thus it appears that there is no peculiar contrariety between self-love and benevolence; no greater competition between
these, than between any other particular affections and self-
love. This relates to the affections themselves. Let us now
see whether there be any peculiar contrariety between the respective courses of life which these affections lead to;
whether there be any greater competition between the pursuit of
private and of public good, than between any other particular
pursuits and that of private good.

There seems no other reason to suspect that there is any
such peculiar contrariety, but only that the course of action
which benevolence leads to, has a more direct tendency to promote the good of others, than that course of action which love
of reputation, suppose, or any other particular affection leads
to. But that any affection tends to the happiness of another,
does not hinder its tending to one's own happiness too. That
others enjoy the benefit of the air and the light of the sun,
does not hinder but that these are as much one's own private
advantage now, as they would be if we had the property of them
exclusive of all others. So a pursuit which tends to promote
the good of another, yet may have as great tendency to promote

private interest, as a pursuit which does not tend to the good
of another at all, or which is mischievous to him. All particular affections whatever, resentment, benevolence, love of arts,
equally lead to a course of action for their own gratification,
i.e. the gratification of ourselves; and the gratification of
each gives delight: so far then it is manifest they have all
the same respect to private interest. Now take into consideration further, concerning these three pursuits, that the end of
the first is the harm, of the second, the good of another, of
the last, somewhat indifferent; and is there any necessity,
that these additional considerations should alter the respect,
which we before saw these three pursuits had to private interest; or render any one of them less conducive to it, than any
other? Thus one man's affection is to honour as his end; in
order to obtain which he thinks no pains too great. Suppose
another with such a singularity of mind, as to have the same
affection to public good as his end, which he endeavours with
the same labour to obtain. In case of success, surely the
man of benevolence hath as great enjoyment as the man of ambition; they both equally having the end of their affections, in
the same degree, tended to: but in case of disappointment, the
benevolent man has clearly the advantage; since endeavouring to
do good considered as a virtuous pursuit, is gratified by its
own consciousness, *i.e.* is in a degree its own reward.

And as to these two, or benevolence and any other particular passions whatever, considered in a further view, as forming
a general temper, which more or less disposes us for enjoyment
of all the common blessings of life, distinct from their own
gratification: is benevolence less the temper of tranquillity
and freedom than ambition or covetousness? Does the benevolent
man appear less easy with himself, from his love to his neighbour? Does he less relish his being? Is there any peculiar
gloom seated on his face? Is his mind less open to entertain-
ment, to any particular gratification? Nothing is more manifest, than that being in good humour, which is benevolence
whilst it lasts, is itself the temper of satisfaction and enjoyment.

Suppose then a man sitting down to consider how he might
become most easy to himself, and attain the greatest pleasure
he could; all that which is his real natural happiness. This
can only consist in the enjoyment of those objects, which are
by nature adapted to our several faculties. These particular
enjoyments make up the sum total of our happiness; and they are
supposed to arise from riches, honours, and the gratification
of sensual appetites. Be it so: yet none profess themselves so
completely happy in these enjoyments, but that there is room
left in the mind for others, if they were presented to them:
nay these, as much as they engage us, are not thought so high,
but that human nature is capable even of greater. Now there

have been persons in all ages, who have professed that they
found satisfaction in the exercise of charity, in the love of
their neighbour, in endeavouring to promote the happiness of
all they had to do with, and in the pursuit of what is just
and right and good, as the general bent of their mind, and end
of their life; and that doing an action of baseness or cruelty
would be as great violence to *their* self, as much breaking in
upon their nature, as any external force. Persons of this
character would add, if they might be heard, that they consider
themselves as acting in the view of an infinite Being, who is
in a much higher sense the object of reverence and of love,
than all the world besides; and therefore they could have no
more enjoyment from a wicked action done under his eye, than
the persons to whom they are making their apology could, if all
mankind were the spectators of it; and that the satisfaction of
approving themselves to his unerring judgment, to whom they
thus refer all their actions, is a more continued settled satisfaction than any this world can afford; as also that they
have, no less than others, a mind free and open to all the common innocent gratifications of it, such as they are. And if we
go no further, does there appear any absurdity in this? Will
any one take upon him to say, that a man cannot find his account in this general course of life, as much as in the most
unbounded ambition, and the excesses of pleasure? Or that such
a person has not consulted so well for himself, for the satisfaction and peace of his own mind, as the ambitious or disso-
lute man? And though the consideration, that God himself will
in the end justify their taste, and support their cause, is not
formally to be insisted upon here; yet thus much comes in, that
all enjoyments whatever are much more clear and unmixed from
the assurance that they will end well. Is it certain then that
there is nothing in these pretensions to happiness? especially
when there are not wanting persons, who have supported themselves with satisfactions of this kind in sickness, poverty,
disgrace, and in the very pangs of death; whereas it is manifest all other enjoyments fail in these circumstances. This
surely looks suspicious of having somewhat in it. Self-love
methinks should be alarmed. May she not possibly pass over
greater pleasures than those she is so wholly taken up with?

The short of the matter is no more than this. Happiness
consists in the gratification of certain affections, appetites,
passions, with objects which are by nature adapted to them.
Self-love may indeed set us on work to gratify these; but happiness or enjoyment has no immediate connection with self-love,
but arises from such gratification alone. Love of our neighbour is one of those affections. This, considered as a *virtuous principle*, is gratified by a consciousness of *endeavouring*
to promote the good of others; but considered as a natural affection, its gratification consists in the actual accomplish-

ment of this endeavour. Now indulgence or gratification of this affection, whether in that consciousness, or this accomplishment, has the same respect to interest, as indulgence of any other affection; they equally proceed from or do not proceed from self-love, they equally include or equally exclude this principle. Thus it appears, that *benevolence and the pursuit of public good hath at least as great respect to self-love and the pursuit of private good, as any other particular passions, and their respective pursuits.*

Neither is covetousness, whether as a temper or pursuit, any exception to this. For if by covetousness is meant the desire and pursuit of riches for their own sake, without any regard to, or consideration of the uses of them; this hath as little to do with self-love, as benevolence hath. But by this word is usually meant, not such madness and total distraction of mind, but immoderate affection to and pursuit of riches as possessions in order to some further end; namely, satisfaction, interest, or good. This therefore is not a particular affection, or particular pursuit, but it is the general principle of self-love, and the general pursuit of our own interest; for which reason, the word selfish is by every one appropriated to this temper and pursuit. Now as it is ridiculous to assert, that self-love and the love of our neighbour are the same; so neither is it asserted, that following these different affections hath the same tendency and respect to our own interest. The comparison is not between self-love and the love of our neighbour; between pursuit of our own interest, and the interest of others: but between the several particular affections in human nature towards external objects, as one part of the comparison; and the one particular affection to the good of our neighbour, as the other part of it: and it has been shewn that all these have the same respect to self-love and private interest.

There is indeed frequently an inconsistence of interfering between self-love or private interest, and the several particular appetites, passions, affections, or the pursuits they lead to. But this competition or interfering is merely accidental; and happens much oftener between pride, revenge, sensual gratifications and private interest, than between private interest and benevolence. For nothing is more common, than to see men give themselves up to a passion or an affection to their known prejudice and ruin, and in direct contradiction to manifest and real interest, and the loudest calls of self-love: whereas the seeming competitions and interfering, between benevolence and private interest, relate much more to the materials or means of enjoyment, than to enjoyment itself. There is often an interfering in the former, when there is none in the latter. Thus as to riches: so much money as a man gives away, so much less will remain in his possession. Here is a real interfering.

But though a man cannot possibly give without lessening his
fortune, yet there are multitudes might give without lessening
their own enjoyment; because they may have more than they can
turn to any real use or advantage to themselves. Thus the more
thought and time any one employs about the interests and good
of others, he must necessarily have less to attend his own; but
he may have so ready and large a supply of his own wants, that
such thought might be really useless to himself, though of
great service and assistance to others.

　　The general mistake, that there is some greater inconsistence between endeavouring to promote the good of another and
self-interest, than between self-interest and pursuing anything
else, seems, as hath already been hinted, to arise from our notions of property; and to be carried on by this property's being supposed to be itself our happiness or good. People are so
very much taken up with this one subject, that they seem from
it to have formed a general way of thinking, which they apply
to other things that they have nothing to do with. Hence, in
a confused and slight way, it might well be taken for granted,
that another's having no interest in an affection (*i.e.* his
good not being the object of it) renders, as one may speak, the
proprietor's interest in it greater; and that if another had an
interest in it, this would render his less, or occasion that
such affection could not be so friendly to self-love, or conducive to private good, as an affection or pursuit which has not
a regard to the good of another. This, I say, might be taken
for granted, whilst it was not attended to, that the object of
every particular affection is equally somewhat external to ourselves; and whether it be the good of another person, or
whether it be any other external thing, makes no alteration
with regard to its being one's own affection, and the gratification of it one's own private enjoyment. And so far as it is
taken for granted, that barely having the means and materials
of enjoyment is what constitutes interest and happiness; that
our interest or good consists in possessions themselves, in
having the property of riches, houses, lands, gardens, not in
the enjoyment of them; so far it will even more strongly be
taken for granted, in the way already explained, that an affection's conducing to the good of another must even necessarily
occasion it to conduce less to private good, if not to be positively detrimental to it. For, if property and happiness are
one and the same thing, as by increasing the property of another, you lessen your own property, so by promoting the happiness of another you must lessen your own happiness. But
whatever occasioned the mistake, I hope it has been fully
proved to be one; as it has been proved, that there is no peculiar rivalship or competition between self-love and benevolence; that as there may be a competition between these two
so there may also between any particular affection whatever
and self-love; that every particular affection, benevolence

among the rest, is subservient to self-love by being the in-
strument of private enjoyment; and that in one respect benevolence contributes more to private interest, *i.e.* enjoyment or
satisfaction, than any other of the particular common affections, as it is in a degree its own gratification.

And to all these things may be added, that religion, from
whence arises our strongest obligation to benevolence, is so
far from disowning the principle of self-love, that it often
addresses itself to that very principle, and always to the mind
in that state when reason presides; and there can no access be
had to the understanding, but by convincing men, that the
course of life we would persuade them to is not contrary to
their interest. It may be allowed, without any prejudice to
the cause of virtue and religion, that our ideas of happiness
and misery are of all our ideas the nearest and most important
to us; that they will, nay, if you please, that they ought to
prevail over those of order, and beauty, and harmony, and proportion, if there should ever be, as it is impossible there
ever should be, any inconsistence between them: though these
last too, as expressing the fitness of actions, are real as
truth itself. Let it be allowed, though virtue or moral recti-
tude does indeed consist in affection to and pursuit of what is
right and good, as such; yet, that when we sit down in a cool
hour, we can neither justify to ourselves this or any other
pursuit, till we are convinced that it will be for our happiness, or at least not contrary to it.

Common reason and humanity will have some influence upon
mankind, whatever becomes of speculations: but, so far as the
interests of virtue depend upon the theory of it being secured
from open scorn, so far its very being in the world depends
upon its appearing to have no contrariety to private interest
and self-love. The foregoing observations therefore, it is
hoped, may have gained a little ground in favour of the precept
before us; the particular explanation of which shall be the
subject of the next Discourse.

I will conclude at present, with observing the peculiar
obligation which we are under to virtue and religion, as en-
forced in the verses following the text, in the epistle for the
day, from our Saviour's coming into the world. *The night is
far spent, the day is at hand; let us therefore cast off the
works of darkness, and let us put on the armour of light, etc.*
The meaning and force of which exhortation is, that Christian-
ity lays us under new obligations to a good life, as by it the
will of God is more clearly revealed, and as it afford additional motives to the practice of it, over and above those
which arise out of the nature of virtue and vice; I might add,
as our Saviour has set us a perfect example of goodness in our
own nature. Now love and charity is plainly the thing in which
he hath placed his religion; in which therefore, as we have any

pretence to the name of Christians, we must place ours. He
hath at once enjoined it upon us by way of command with peculiar force; and by his example, as having undertaken the work
of our salvation out of pure love and good-will to mankind.
The endeavour to set home this example upon our minds is a very
proper employment of this season, which is bringing on the
festival of his birth: which as it may teach us many excellent
lessons of humility, resignation and obedience to the will of
God, so there is none it recommends with greater authority,
force and advantage, than this of love and charity; since it
was *for us men, and for our salvation,* that *he came down from
heaven, and was incarnate, and was made man*; that he might
teach us our duty, and more especially that he might enforce
the practice of it, reform mankind, and finally bring us to
that *eternal salvation,* of which *he is the Author to all those
that obey him.*

David Hume

MORALITY, SELF-LOVE, AND BENEVOLENCE

From *An Enquiry Concerning the Principles of Morals*
(1751). Reprinted here are selections from Section 5
("Why Utility Pleases"), Section 6 ("Of Qualities Useful to Ourselves"), and Section 9 ("Conclusion"). De-
letions are indicated, and some footnotes have also
been omitted. David Hume (1711-76) made significant
and lasting contributions to almost every branch of
philosophy—epistemology, metaphysics, ethics, politi-
cal philosophy, philosophy of religion, and aesthetics.
Among the more important of his writings are: *Treatise
of Human Nature, Enquiry Concerning Human Understanding,* and *Dialogues Concerning Natural Religion.*

It seems so natural a thought to ascribe to their utility
the praise which we bestow on the social virtues, that one
would expect to meet with this principle everywhere in moral
writers, as the chief foundation of their reasoning and inquiry. In common life, we may observe, that the circumstance
of utility is always appealed to; nor is it supposed that a
greater eulogy can be given to any man, than to display his
usefulness to the public, and enumerate the services which he

has performed to mankind and to society. What praise, even of
an inanimate form, if the regularity and elegance of its parts
destroy not its fitness for any useful purpose! And how satisfactory an apology for any disproportion or seeming deformity,
if we can show the necessity of that particular construction
for the use intended! A ship appears more beautiful to an
artist, or one moderately skilled in navigation, where its prow
is wide and swelling beyond its poop, than if it were framed
with a precise geometrical regularity, in contradiction to all
the laws of mechanics. A building, whose doors and windows
were exact squares, would hurt the eye by that very proportion,
as ill adapted to the figure of a human creature, for whose
service the fabric was intended. What wonder then that a man,
whose habits and conduct are hurtful to society, and dangerous
and pernicious to every one who has intercourse with him,
should, on that account, be an object of disapprobation, and
communicate to every spectator the strongest sentiment of disgust and hatred?

But perhaps the difficulty of accounting for these effects
of usefulness, or its contrary, has kept philosophers from ad-
mitting them into their systems of ethics, and has induced them
rather to employ any other principle, in explaining the origin
of moral good and evil. But it is no just reason for rejecting
any principle, confirmed by experience, that we cannot give a
satisfactory account of its origin, nor are able to resolve into other more general principles. And if we would employ a
little thought on the present subject, we need be at no loss to
account for the influence of utility, and to deduce it from
principles, the most known and avowed in human nature.

From the apparent usefulness of the social virtues, it has
readily been inferred by sceptics, both ancient and modern,
that all moral distinctions arise from education, and were at
first invented, and afterwards encouraged, by the art of politicians, in order to render men tractable, and subdue their
natural ferocity and selfishness, which incapacitated them for
society. This principle, indeed, of precept and education,
must so far be owned to have a powerful influence, that it may
frequently increase or diminish, beyond their natural standard,
the sentiments of approbation or dislike; and may even, in particular instances, create, without any natural principle, a new
sentiment of this kind, as it is evident in all superstitious
practices and observances: but that *all* moral affection or dislike arises from this origin, will never surely be allowed by
any judicious inquirer. Had nature made no such distinction,
founded on the original constitution of the mind, the words
honorable and *shameful, lovely* and *odious, noble* and *despicable*,
had never any place in any language; nor could politicians, had
they invented these terms, ever have been able to render them
intelligible, or make them convey an idea to the audience. So

that nothing can be more superficial than this paradox of the sceptics; and it were well if, in the abstruser studies of logic and metaphysics, we could as easily obviate the cavils of that sect, as in the practical and more intelligible sciences of politics and morals.

The social virtues must, therefore, be allowed to have a natural beauty and amiableness, which at first, antecedent to all precept or education, recommends them to the esteem of un-instructed mankind, and engages their affections. And as the public utility of these virtues is the chief circumstance whence they derive their merit, it follows, that the end, which they have a tendency to promote, must be some way agreeable to us, and take hold of some natural affection. It must please, either from considerations of self-interest, or from more gen-erous motives and regards.

It has often been asserted, that as every man has a strong connection with society, and perceives the impossibility of his solitary subsistence, he becomes, on that account, favorable to all those habits or principles which promote order in society, and insure to him the quiet possession of so inestimable a blessing. As much as we value our own happiness and welfare, as much must we applaud the practice of justice and humanity, by which alone the social confederacy can be maintained, and every man reap the fruits of mutual protection and assistance.

This deduction of morals from self-love, or a regard to private interest, is an obvious thought, and has not arisen wholly from the wanton sallies and sportive assaults of the sceptics. To mention no others, Polybius, one of the gravest and most judicious, as well as most moral writers of antiquity, has assigned the selfish origin to all our sentiments of virtue. But though the solid practical sense of that author, and his aversion to all vain subtilties, render his authority on the present subject very considerable, yet is not this an affair to be decided by authority; and the voice of nature and experience seems plainly to oppose the selfish theory.

We frequently bestow praise on virtuous actions, performed in very distant ages and remote countries, where the utmost subtilty of imagination would not discover any appearance of self-interest, or find any connection of our present happiness and security with events so widely separated from us.

A generous, a brave, a noble deed, performed by an adver-sary, commands our approbation; while, in its consequences, it may be acknowledged prejudicial to our particular interest.

When private advantage concurs, with general affection for virtue, we readily perceive and avow the mixture of these dis-tinct sentiments, which have a very different feeling and in-fluence on the mind. We praise, perhaps, with more alacrity, where the generous, humane action, contributes to our particu-lar interest: but the topics of praise, which we insist on, are

very wide of this circumstance. And we may attempt to bring
over others to our sentiments, without endeavoring to convince
them that they reap any advantage from the actions which we
recommend to their approbation and applause.

Frame the model of a praiseworthy character, consisting of
all the most amiable moral virtues: give instances in which
these display themselves after an eminent and extraordinary
manner: you readily engage the esteem and approbation of all
your audience, who never so much as inquire in what age and
country the person lived who possessed these noble qualities;
a circumstance, however, of all others the most material to
self-love, or a concern for our own individual happiness.

Once on a time a statesman, in the shock and contest of
parties, prevailed so far as to procure, by his eloquence, the
banishment of an able adversary; whom he secretly followed, of-
fering him money for his support during his exile, and soothing
him with topics of consolation in his misfortunes. *Alas*! cries
the banished statesman, *with what regret must I leave my
friends in this city, where even enemies are so dangerous*!
Virtue, though in an enemy, here pleased him: and we also give
it the just tribute of praise and approbation; nor do we re-
tract these sentiments, when we hear that the action passed at
Athens about two thousand years ago, and that the persons'
names were Eschines and Demosthenes.

What is that to me? There are few occasions when this
question is not pertinent: and had it that universal, infallible influence supposed, it would turn into ridicule every compo-
sition, and almost every conversation, which contain any praise
or censure of men and manners.

It is but a weak subterfuge, when pressed by these facts
and arguments, to say that we transport ourselves, by the force
of imagination, into distant ages and countries, and consider
the advantage which we should have reaped from these characters
had we been contemporaries, and had any commerce with the persons. It is not conceivable how a *real* sentiment or passion
can ever arise from a known *imaginary* interest, especially when
our *real* interest is still kept in view, and is often acknowledged to be entirely distinct from the imaginary, and even
sometimes opposite to it.

A man brought to the brink of a precipice, cannot look
down without trembling; and the sentiment of *imaginary* danger
actuates him, in opposition to the opinion and belief of *real*
safety. But the imagination is here assisted by the presence
of a striking object, and yet prevails not, except it be also
aided by novelty, and the unusual appearance of the object.
Custom soon reconciles us to heights and precipices, and wears
off these false and delusive terrors. The reverse is observable in the estimates which we form of characters and manners;
and the more we habituate ourselves to an accurate scrutiny of

morals, the more delicate feeling do we acquire of the most
minute distinctions between vice and virtue. Such frequent
occasion, indeed, have we, in common life, to pronounce all
kinds of moral determinations, that no object of this kind can
be new or unusual to us; nor could any *false* views or prepos-
sessions maintain their ground against an experience so common
and familiar. Experience being chiefly what forms the associ-
ations of ideas, it is impossible that any association could
establish and support itself in direct opposition to that
principle.

Usefulness is agreeable, and engages our approbation.
This is a matter of fact, confirmed by daily observation. But
useful? For what? For somebody's interest surely. Whose interest then? Not our own only, for our approbation frequently
extends further. It must therefore be the interest of those
who are served by the character or action approved of; and
these, we may conclude, however remote, are not totally indifferent to us. By opening up this principle, we shall discover
one great source of moral distinctions.

Self-love is a principle in human nature of such extensive
energy, and the interest of each individual is in general so
closely connected with that of the community, that those philosophers were excusable who fancied that all our concern for
the public might be resolved into a concern for our own happiness and preservation. They saw, every moment, instances of
approbation or blame, satisfaction or displeasure, towards
characters and actions; they denominated the objects of these
sentiments *virtues* or *vices*; they observed, that the former had
a tendency to increase the happiness, and the latter the misery
of mankind; they asked, whether it were possible that we could
have any general concern for society, or any disinterested resentment of the welfare or injury of others; they found it simp-
ler to consider all these sentiments as modifications of self-
love; and they discovered a pretence at least for this unity of
principle, in that close union of interest which is so observable between the public and each individual.

But notwithstanding this frequent confusion of interests,
it is easy to attain what natural philosophers, after Lord
Bacon, have affected to call the *experimentum crucis*, or that
experiment which points out the right way in any doubt or am-
biguity. We have found instances in which private interest was
separate from public; in which it was even contrary, and yet we
observed the moral sentiment to continue, notwithstanding this
disjunction of interests. And wherever these distinct interests sensibly concurred, we always found a sensible increase of
the sentiment, and a more warm affection to virtue, and detesta-
tion of vice, or what we properly call *gratitude* and *revenge*.
Compelled by these instances, we must renounce the theory which
accounts for every moral sentiment by the principle of self-

love. We must adopt a more public affection, and allow that
the interests of society are not, even on their own account,
entirely indifferent to us. Usefulness is only a tendency to
a certain end; and it is a contradiction in terms, that any
thing pleases as means to an end, where the end itself nowise
affects us. If usefulness, therefore, be a source of moral
sentiment, and if this usefulness be not always considered
with a reference to self, it follows, that every thing which
contributes to the happiness of society recommends itself directly to our approbation and good-will. Here is a principle
which accounts, in great part, for the origin of morality: and
what need we seek for abstruse and remote systems, when there
occurs one so obvious and natural?[1]

Have we any difficulty to comprehend the force of humanity
and benevolence? Or to conceive, that the very aspect of happiness, joy, prosperity, gives pleasure; that of pain, suffering, sorrow, communicates uneasiness? The human countenance,
says Horace, borrows smiles or tears from the human countenance. Reduce a person to solitude, and he loses all enjoyment, except either of the sensual or speculative kind; and
that because the movements of his heart are not forwarded by
correspondent movements in his fellow-creatures. The signs of
sorrow and mourning, though arbitrary, affect us with melancholy; but the natural symptoms, tears, and cries, and groans,
never fail to infuse compassion and uneasiness. And if the
effects of misery touch us in so lively a manner, can we be
supposed altogether insensible or indifferent towards its
causes, when a malicious or treacherous character and behavior
are presented to us?

We enter, I shall suppose, into a convenient, warm, well-
contrived apartment: we necessarily receive a pleasure from its
very survey, because it presents us with the pleasing ideas of

---

[1]It is needless to push our researches so far as to ask, why
we have humanity or a fellow-feeling with others? It is sufficient that this is experienced to be a principle in human nature. We must stop somewhere in our examination of causes; and
there are, in every science, some general principles, beyond
which we cannot hope to find any principle more general. No
man is absolutely indifferent to the happiness and misery of
others. The first has a natural tendency to give pleasure, the
second pain. This every one may find in himself. It is not
probable that these principles can be resolved into principles
more simple and universal, whatever attempts may have been made
to that purpose. But if it were possible, it belongs not to
the present subject; and we may here safely consider these principles as original,—happy if we can render all the consequences
sufficiently plain and perspicuous!

ease, satisfaction, and enjoyment. The hospitable, good-
humored, humane landlord appears. This circumstance surely
must embellish the whole; nor can we easily forbear reflecting,
with pleasure, on the satisfaction which results to every one
from his intercourse and good offices.

His whole family, by the freedom, ease, confidence, and
calm enjoyment diffused over their countenances, sufficiently
express their happiness. I have a pleasing sympathy in the
prospect of so much joy, and can never consider the source of
it without the most agreeable emotions.

He tells me that an oppressive and powerful neighbor had
attempted to dispossess him of his inheritance, and had long
disturbed all his innocent and social pleasures. I feel an
immediate indignation arise in me against such violence and
injury.

But it is no wonder, he adds, that a private wrong should
proceed from a man who had enslaved provinces, depopulated
cities, and made the field and scaffold stream with human
blood. I am struck with horror at the prospect of so much
misery, and am actuated by the strongest antipathy against its
author.

In general, it is certain, that wherever we go, whatever
we reflect on or converse about, every thing still presents us
with the view of human happiness or misery, and excites in our
breast a sympathetic movement of pleasure or uneasiness. In
our serious occupations, in our careless amusements, this
principle still exerts its active energy. . . .

The more we converse with mankind, and the greater social
intercourse we maintain, the more shall we be familiarized to
these general preferences and distinctions, without which our
conversation and discourse could scarcely be rendered intelligible to each other. Every man's interest is peculiar to himself, and the aversions and desires which result from it cannot
be supposed to affect others in a like degree. General language therefore, being formed for general use, must be moulded
on more general views, and must affix the epithets of praise or
blame, in conformity to sentiments which arise from the general
interests of the community. And if these sentiments, in most
men, be not so strong as those which have a reference to private good, yet still they must make some distinction, even in
persons the most depraved and selfish, and must attach the notion of good to a beneficent conduct, and of evil to the contrary. Sympathy, we shall allow, is much fainter than our
concern for ourselves, and sympathy with persons remote from us
much fainter than that with persons near and contiguous; but
for this very reason, it is necessary for us, in our calm judgments and discourse concerning the characters of men, to neglect all the differences, and render our sentiments more
public and social. Besides, that we ourselves often change our

situation in this particular, we every day meet with persons who are in a situation different from us, and who could never converse with us, were we to remain constantly in that position and point of view which is peculiar to ourselves. The intercourse of sentiments, therefore, in society and conversation, make us form some general unalterable standard, by which we may approve or disapprove of characters and manners. And though the heart takes not part entirely with those general notions, nor regulates all its love and hatred by the universal abstract differences of vice and virtue, without regard to self, or the persons with whom we are more intimately connected, yet have these moral differences a considerable influence; and being sufficient, at least, for discourse, serve all our purposes in company, in the pulpit, in the theatre, and in the schools.[2]

Thus, in whatever light we take this subject, the merit ascribed to the social virtues appears still uniform, and arises chiefly from that regard which the natural sentiment of benevolence engages us to pay to the interests of mankind and society. If we consider the principles of the human make, such as they appear to daily experience and observation, we must, *à priori*, conclude it impossible for such a creature as man to be totally indifferent to the well or ill being of his fellow-creatures, and not readily, of himself, to pronounce, where nothing gives him any particular bias, that what promotes their happiness is good, what tends to their misery is evil, without any further regard or consideration. Here then are the faint rudiments at least, or outlines, of a *general* distinction between actions; and in proportion as the humanity of the person is supposed to increase, his connection with those who are injured or benefited, and his lively conception of their misery or happiness, his consequent censure or approbation acquires proportionable vigor. There is no necessity that a generous action, barely mentioned in an old history or remote gazette, should communicate any strong feelings of applause and admiration. Virtue, placed at such a distance, is like a fixed star, which, though to the eye of reason it may appear as luminous as the sun in his meridian, is so infinitely removed as to affect

---

[2]It is wisely ordained by nature, that private connections should commonly prevail over universal views and considerations, otherwise our affections and actions would be dissipated and lost for want of a proper limited object. Thus a small benefit done to ourselves, or our near friends, excites more lively sentiments of love and approbation, than a great benefit done to a distant commonwealth: but still we know here, as in all the senses, to correct these inequalities by reflection, and retain a general standard of vice and virtue, founded chiefly on general usefulness.

the senses neither with light nor heat. Bring this virtue
nearer, by our acquaintance or connection with the persons, or
even by an eloquent recital of the case, our hearts are immediately caught, our sympathy enlivened, and our cool approbation
converted into the warmest sentiments of friendship and regard.
These seem necessary and infallible consequences of the general
principles of human nature, as discovered in common life and
practice.

Again, reverse these views and reasonings: consider the
matter *à posteriori*; and, weighing the consequences, inquire if
the merit of social virtue be not, in a great measure, derived
from the feelings of humanity with which it affects the spectators. It appears to be matter of fact, that the circumstance
of *utility*, in all subjects, is a source of praise and approbation: that it is constantly appealed to in all moral decisions
concerning the merit and demerit of actions: that it is the
sole source of that high regard paid to justice, fidelity, hon-
or, allegiance, and chastity: that it is inseparable from all
the other social virtues, humanity, generosity, charity, affa-
bility, lenity, mercy, and moderation: and, in a word, it is a
foundation of the chief part of morals, which has a reference
to mankind and our fellow-creatures.

It appears also that, in our general approbation of characters and manners, the useful tendency of the social virtues
moves us not by any regards to self-interest, but has an influence much more universal and extensive. It appears that a
tendency to public good, and to the promoting of peace, harmony, and order in society, does always, by affecting the benevolent principles of our frame, engage us on the side of the
social virtues. And it appears, as an additional confirmation,
that these principles of humanity and sympathy enter so deeply
into all our sentiments, and have so powerful an influence, as
may enable them to excite the strongest censure and applause.
The present theory is the simple result of all these inferences,
each of which seems founded on uniform experience and observation.

Were it doubtful whether there were any such principle in
our nature as humanity or a concern for others, yet when we
see, in numberless instances, that whatever has a tendency to
promote the interest of society, is so highly approved of, we
ought thence to learn the force of the benevolent principle,
since it is impossible for any thing to please as means to an
end, where the end is totally indifferent. On the other hand,
were it doubtful whether there were implanted in our nature any
general principle of moral blame and approbation, yet when we
see, in numberless instances, the influence of humanity, we
ought thence to conclude, that it is impossible but that every
thing which promotes the interests of society must communicate
pleasure, and what is pernicious give uneasiness. But when

these different reflections and observations concur in estab-
lishing the same conclusion, must they not bestow an undis-
puted evidence upon it? . . .

It seems evident, that where a quality or habit is sub-
jected to our examination, if it appear in any respect prejudicial to the person possessed of it, or such as incapacitates
him for business and action, it is instantly blamed, and ranked
among his faults and imperfections. Indolence, negligence,
want of order and method, obstinacy, fickleness, rashness, cre-
dulity; these qualities were never esteemed by any one indifferent to a character, much less extolled as accomplishments or
virtues. The prejudice resulting from them immediately strikes
our eye, and gives us the sentiment of pain and disapprobation.

No quality, it is allowed, is absolutely either blamable
or praiseworthy. It is all according to its degree. A due
medium, says the PERIPATETICS, is the characteristic of virtue.
But this medium is chiefly determined by utility. A proper
celerity, for instance, and despatch in business, is commendable. When defective, no progress is ever made in the execu-
tion of any purpose. When excessive, it engages us in precipi-
tate and ill-concerted measures and enterprises: by such
reasonings we fix the proper and commendable mediocrity in all
moral and prudential disquisitions; and never lose view of the
advantages which result from any character or habit.

Now, as these advantages are enjoyed by the person possessed of the character, it can never be *self-love* which renders the prospect of them agreeable to us, the spectators, and
prompts our esteem and approbation. No force of imagination
can convert us into another person, and make us fancy that we,
being that person, reap benefit from those valuable qualities
which belong to him. Or if it did, no celerity of imagination
could immediately transport us back into ourselves, and make us
love and esteem the person as different from us. Views and
sentiments so opposite to known truth, and to each other, could
never have place, at the same time, in the same person. All
suspicion, therefore, of selfish regards is here totally excluded.

It is a quite different principle which actuates our bosom,
and interests us in the felicity of the person whom we contemplate. Where his natural talents and acquired abilities give
us the prospect of elevation, advancement, a figure in life,
prosperous success, a steady command over fortune, and the exe-
cution of great or advantageous undertakings; we are struck
with such agreeable images, and feel a complacency and regard
immediately arise towards him.[3] The ideas of happiness, joy,

---

[3]One may venture to affirm, that there is no human creature, to
whom the appearance of happiness (where envy or revenge has no

triumph, prosperity, are connected with every circumstance of
his character, and diffuse over our minds a pleasing sentiment
of sympathy and humanity.
      Let us suppose a person originally framed so as to have no
manner of concern for his fellow-creatures, but to regard the
happiness and misery of all sensible beings with greater indifference than even two contiguous shades of the same color. Let
us suppose, if the prosperity of nations were laid on the one
hand, and their ruin on the other, and he were desired to
choose; that he would stand like the schoolman's ass, irreso-
lute and undetermined between equal motives; or rather, like
the same ass between two pieces of wood or marble, without any
inclination or propensity to either side. The consequence, I
believe, must be allowed just, that such a person, being absolutely unconcerned, either for the public good of a community,
or the private utility of others, would look on every quality,
however pernicious, or however beneficial to society, or to its
possessor, with the same indifference as on the most common and
uninteresting object.
      But if, instead of this fancied monster, we suppose a *man*
to form a judgment or determination in the case, there is to
him a plain foundation of preference, where every thing else is
equal; and, however cool his choice may be, if his heart be
selfish, or if the persons interested be remote from him, there
must still be a choice or distinction between what is useful
and what is pernicious. Now, this distinction is the same, in
all its parts, with the *moral distinction* whose foundation has
been so often, and so much in vain, inquired after. The same
endowments of the mind, in every circumstance, are agreeable to
the sentiment of morals and to that of humanity; the same temper is susceptible of high degrees of the one sentiment and of

---

[3](cont.) place), does not give pleasure; that of misery, uneasiness. This seems inseparable from our make and constitution. But they are only the more generous minds that are
thence prompted to seek zealously the good of others, and to
have a real passion for their welfare. With men of narrow and
ungenerous spirits, this sympathy goes not beyond a slight feeling of the imagination, which serves only to excite sentiments
of complacency or censure, and makes them apply to the object
either honorable or dishonorable appellations. A griping miser,
for instance, praises extremely *industry* and *frugality* even in
others, and sets them, in his estimation, above all the other
virtues. He knows the good that results from them, and feels
that species of happiness with a more lively sympathy, than any
other you could represent to him; though perhaps he would not
part with a shilling to make the fortune of the industrious man
whom he praises so highly.

the other; and the same alteration in the objects, by their
nearer approach or by connections, enlivens the one and the
other. By all the rules of philosophy, therefore, we must conclude, that these sentiments are originally the same; since, in
each particular, even the most minute, they are governed by the
same laws, and are moved by the same objects. . . .

In this kingdom, such continued ostentation, of late years,
has prevailed among men in *active* life with regard to *public
spirit*, and among those in *speculative* with regard to *benevolence*, and so many false pretensions to each have been no doubt
detected, that men of the world are apt, without any bad intention, to discover a sullen incredulity on the head of those
moral endowments, and even sometimes absolutely to deny their
existence and reality. In like manner, I find that of old the
perpetual cant of the *Stoics* and *Cynics* concerning *virtue*,
their magnificent professions and slender performances, bred a
disgust in mankind; and Lucian, who, though licentious with regard to pleasure, is yet, in other respects, a very moral writ-
er, cannot sometimes talk of virtue, so much boasted, without
betraying symptoms of spleen and irony. But surely this pee-
vish delicacy, whencesoever it arises, can never be carried so
far as to make us deny the existence of every species of merit,
and all distinction of manners and behavior. Besides *discre-
tion, caution, enterprise, industry, assiduity, frugality,
economy, good sense, prudence, discernment*; besides these endowments, I say, whose very names force an avowal of their
merit, there are many others to which the most determined scepticism cannot for a moment refuse the tribute of praise and approbation. *Temperance, sobriety, patience, constancy, perse-
verence, forethought, considerateness, secrecy, order, insinu-
ation, address, presence of mind, quickness of conception, fa-
cility of expression*; these, and a thousand more of the same
kind, no man will ever deny to be excellences and perfections.
As their merit consists in their tendency to serve the person
possessed of them, without any magnificent claim to public and
social desert, we are the less jealous of their pretensions,
and readily admit them into the catalogue of laudable qualities.
We are not sensible, that, by this concession, we have paved
the way for all the other moral excellences, and cannot consistently hesitate any longer, with regard to disinterested benevolence, patriotism, and humanity.

It seems, indeed, certain, that first appearances are
here, as usual, extremely deceitful, and that it is more difficult, in a speculative way, to resolve self-love into the merit
which we ascribe to the selfish virtues above mentioned, than
that even of the social virtues, justice and beneficence. For
this latter purpose, we need but say, that whatever conduct promotes the good of the community, is loved, praised, and esteemed by the community, on account of that utility and interest

of which every one partakes: and though this affection and regard be, in reality, gratitude, not self-love, yet a distinction, even of this obvious nature, may not readily be made by
superficial reasoners; and there is room at least to support
the cavil and dispute for a moment. But as qualities which
tend only to the utility of their possessor, without any reference to us, or to the community, are yet esteemed and valued,
by what theory or system can we account for this sentiment from
self-love, or deduce it from that favorite origin? There seems
here a necessity for confessing that the happiness and misery
of others are not spectacles entirely indifferent to us, but
that the view of the former, whether in its causes or effects,
like sunshine, or the prospect of well-cultivated plains (to
carry our pretensions no higher), communicates a secret joy and
satisfaction; the appearance of the latter, like a lowering
cloud or barren landscape, throws a melancholy damp over the
imagination. And this concession being once made, the difficulty is over; and a natural unforced interpretation of the
phenomena of human life will afterwards, we hope, prevail among
all speculative inquirers. . . .
    It seems a happiness in the present theory, that it enters
not into that vulgar dispute concerning the *degrees* of benevolence or self-love, which prevail in human nature; a dispute
which is never likely to have any issue; both because men, who
have taken part, are not easily convinced, and because the phenomena, which can be produced on either side, are so dispersed,
so uncertain, and subject to so many interpretations, that it
is scarcely possible accurately to compare them, or draw from
them any determinate inference or conclusion. It is sufficient
for our present purpose, if it be allowed, what surely, without
the greatest absurdity, cannot be disputed, that there is some
benevolence, however small, infused into our bosom; some spark
of friendship for human kind; some particle of the dove kneaded
into our frame, along with the elements of the wolf and serpent.
Let these generous sentiments be supposed ever so weak; let
them be insufficient to move even a hand or finger of our body;
they must still direct the determinations of our mind, and
where every thing else is equal, produce a cool preference of
what is useful and serviceable to mankind above what is pernicious and dangerous. A *moral distinction*, therefore, immediately arises; a general sentiment of blame and approbation; a
tendency, however faint, to the objects of the one, and a proportionable aversion to those of the other. Nor will those
reasoners, who so earnestly maintain the predominant selfishness of human kind, be anywise scandalized at hearing of the
weak sentiments of virtue implanted in our nature. On the contrary, they are found as ready to maintain the one tenet as the
other; and their spirit of satire (for such it appears, rather
than of corruption) naturally gives rise to both opinions;

which have, indeed, a great and almost indissoluble connection together.

Avarice, ambition, vanity, and all passions vulgarly, though improperly, comprised under the denomination of *self-love*, are here excluded from our theory concerning the origin of morals, not because they are too weak, but because they have not a proper direction for that purpose. The notion of morals implies some sentiment common to all mankind, which recommends the same object to general approbation, and makes every man, or most men, agree in the same opinion or decision concerning it. It also implies some sentiment, so universal and comprehensive, as to extend to all mankind, and render the actions and conduct, even of the persons the most remote, an object of applause or censure, according as they agree or disagree with that rule of right which is established. These two requisite circumstances belong alone to the sentiment of humanity here insisted on. The other passions produce, in every breast, many strong sentiments of desire and aversion, affection and hatred; but these neither are felt so much in common, nor are so comprehensive, as to be the foundation of any general system and established theory of blame or approbation.

When a man denominates another his *enemy*, his *rival*, his *antagonist*, his *adversary*, he is understood to speak the language of self-love, and to express sentiments peculiar to himself, and arising from his particular circumstances and situation. But when he bestows on any man the epithets of *vicious*, or *odious*, or *depraved*, he then speaks another language, and expresses sentiments in which he expects all his audience are to concur with him. He must here, therefore, depart from his private and particular situation, and must choose a point of view common to him with others: he must move some universal principle of the human frame, and touch a string to which all mankind have an accord and symphony. If he mean, therefore, to express, that this man possesses qualities, whose tendency is pernicious to society, he has chosen this common point of view, and has touched the principle of humanity, in which every man, in some degree, concurs. While the human heart is compounded of the same elements as at present, it will never be wholly indifferent to public good, nor entirely unaffected with the tendency of characters and manners. And though this affection of humanity may not generally be esteemed so strong as vanity or ambition, yet, being common to all men, it can alone be the foundation of morals, or of any general system of blame or praise. One man's ambition is not another's ambition; nor will the same event or object satisfy both: but the humanity of one man is the humanity of every one; and the same object touches the passion in all human creatures.

But the sentiments which arise from humanity, are not only the same in all human creatures, and produce the same approba-

tion or censure, but they also comprehend all human creatures;
nor is there any one whose conduct or character, is not, by
their means, an object, to every one, of censure or approbation.
On the contrary, those other passions, commonly denominated
selfish, both produce different sentiments in each individual,
according to his particular situation, and also contemplate the
greater part of mankind with the utmost indifference and uncon-
cern. Whoever has a high regard and esteem for me, flatters my
vanity; whoever expresses contempt, mortifies and displeases
me: but as my name is known but to a small part of mankind,
there are few who come within the sphere of this passion, or
excite, on its account, either my affection or disgust. But if
you represent a tyrannical, insolent, or barbarous behavior, in
any country or in any age of the world, I soon carry my eye to
the pernicious tendency of such a conduct, and feel the sentiment of repugnance and displeasure towards it. No character
can be so remote as to be, in this light, wholly indifferent to
me. What is beneficial to society or to the person himself,
must still be preferred. And every quality or action, of every
human being, must, by this means, be ranked under some class or
denomination, expressive of general censure or applause.
       What more, therefore, can we ask to distinguish the senti-
ments dependent on humanity, from those connected with any
other passion, or to satisfy us why the former are the origin
of morals, not the latter? Whatever conduct gains my approbation, by touching my humanity, procures also the applause of
all mankind, by affecting the same principle in them: but what
serves my avarice or ambition pleases these passions in me
alone, and affects not the avarice and ambition of the rest of
mankind. There is no circumstance of conduct in any man, provided it have a beneficial tendency, that is not agreeable to
my humanity, however remote the person: but every man, so far
removed as neither to cross nor serve my avarice and ambition,
is regarded as wholly indifferent by those passions. The distinction, therefore, between these species of sentiment being
so great and evident, language must soon be moulded upon it,
and must invent a peculiar set of terms, in order to express
those universal sentiments of censure or approbation which
arise from humanity, or from views of general usefulness and
its contrary. VIRTUE and VICE become then known: morals are
recognized: certain general ideas are framed of human conduct
and behavior: such measures are expected from men in such situations: this action is determined to be conformable to our abstract rule; that other, contrary. And by such universal principles are the particular sentiments of self-love frequently
controlled and limited.[4] . . .

[4]It seems certain, both from reason and experience, that a rude
untaught savage regulates chiefly his love and hatred by the

Immanuel Kant

MORALITY AND THE DUTY OF LOVE TOWARD OTHER MEN

Reprinted here are selections from *Fundamental Principles of the Metaphysic of Morals* (1785), in the
section I have subheaded "The Moral Law"; from *Critique
of Practical Reason* (1788), in the section subheaded
"Self-Love and Respect for the Moral Law"; and from
The Doctrine of Virtue (Part 2 of *The Metaphysic of
Morals*, 1797), in the section subheaded "The Duty of
Love toward Other Men." Selections from the first
two works were translated by T. K. Abbott. Selections
from *The Doctrine of Virtue* were translated by Mary J.
Gregor. Reprinted here are pp. 46-47, 53-54, 62-63,
and 115-127 from the Harper Torchbook edition (New
York, 1964; copyright 1964 by Mary J. Gregor) by permission of Harper and Row, Publishers, Inc. Kant's
own subheadings have been omitted. In addition to
his writings in the field of ethics, Immanuel Kant
(1724-1804) is famous for his *Critique of Pure Reason*,
one of the major works in metaphysics and epistemology.

[4](cont.) ideas of private utility and injury, and has but faint
conceptions of a general rule or system of behavior. The man
who stands opposite to him in battle he hates heartily, not
only for the present moment, which is almost unavoidable, but
for ever after; nor is he satisfied without the most extreme
punishment and vengeance. But we, accustomed to society, and
to more enlarged reflections, consider that this man is serving
his own country and community; that any man, in the same situation, would do the same; that we ourselves, in like circumstances, observe a like conduct; that, in general, human society is best supported on such maxims. And by these supposi-
tions and views, we correct, in some measure, our ruder and
narrower passions. And though much of our friendship and
enmity be still regulated by private considerations of benefit
and harm, we pay at least this homage to general rules, which
we are accustomed to respect, that we commonly pervert our adversary's conduct, by imputing malice or injustice to him, in
order to give vent to those passions which arise from self-love
and private interest. When the heart is full of rage, it never
wants preferences of this nature, though sometimes as frivolous
as those from which Horace, being almost crushed by the fall of
a tree, affects to accuse of parricide the first planter of it.

THE MORAL LAW

. . . Everything in nature works according to laws. Rational beings alone have the faculty of acting according *to the conception* of laws, that is according to principles, *i.e.* have a *will*. Since the deduction of actions from principles requires *reason*, the will is nothing but practical reason. If reason infallibly determines the will, then the actions of such a being which are recognized as objectively necessary are subjectively necessary also, *i.e.* the will is a faculty to choose *that only* which reason independent on inclination recognizes as practically necessary, *i.e.* as good. But if reason of itself does not sufficiently determine the will, if the latter is subject also to subjective conditions (particular impulses) which do not always coincide with the objective conditions; in a word, if the will does not *in itself* completely accord with reason (which is actually the case with men), then the actions which objectively are recognized as necessary are subjectively contingent, and the determination of such a will according to objective laws is *obligation*, that is to say, the relation of the objective laws to a will that is not thoroughly good is conceived as the determination of the will of a rational being by principles of reason, but which the will from its nature does not of necessity follow.

The conception of an objective principle, in so far as it is obligatory for a will, is called a command (of reason), and the formula of the command is called an Imperative.

All imperatives are expressed by the word *ought* [or shall], and thereby indicate the relation of an objective law of reason to a will, which from its subjective constitution is not necessarily determined by it (an obligation). They say that something would be good to do or to forbear, but they say it to a will which does not always do a thing because it is conceived to be good to do it. That is practically *good*, however, which determines the will by means of the conceptions of reason, and consequently not from subjective causes, but objectively, that is on principles which are valid for every rational being as such. It is distinguished from the *pleasant*, as that which influences the will only by means of sensation from merely subjective causes, valid only for the sense of this or that one, and not as a principle of reason, which holds for every one.[1]

---

[1]The dependence of the desires on sensations is called inclination, and this accordingly always indicates a *want*. The dependence of a contingently determinable will on principles of reason is called an *interest*. This, therefore, is found only in the case of a dependent will which does not always of itself conform to reason; in the Divine will we cannot conceive any

A perfectly good will would therefore be equally subject to objective laws (viz. laws of good), but could not be conceived as *obliged* thereby to act lawfully, because of itself from its subjective constitution it can only be determined by the conception of good. Therefore no imperatives hold for the Divine will, or in general for a *holy* will; *ought* is here out of place, because the volition is already of itself necessarily in unison with the law. Therefore imperatives are only formulae to express the relation of objective laws of all volition to the subjective imperfection of the will of this or that rational being, *e.g.* the human will.

Now all *imperatives* command either *hypothetically* or *categorically*. The former represent the practical necessity of a possible action as means to something else that is willed (or at least which one might possibly will). The categorical imperative would be that which represented an action as necessary of itself without reference to another end, *i.e.*, as objectively necessary.

Since every practical law represents a possible action as good, and on this account, for a subject who is practically determinable by reason, necessary, all imperatives are formulae determining an action which is necessary according to the principle of a will good in some respects. If now the action is good only as a means *to something else*, then the imperative is *hypothetical*; if it is conceived as good *in itself* and consequently as being necessarily the principle of a will which of itself conforms to reason, then it is *categorical*. . . .

When I conceive a hypothetical imperative, in general I do not know beforehand what it will contain until I am given the condition. But when I conceive a categorical imperative, I know at once what it contains. For as the imperative con-

---

[1](cont.) interest. But the human will can also *take an interest* in a thing without therefore acting *from* interest. The former signifies the *practical* interest in the action, the latter the *pathological* in the object of the action. The former indicates only dependence of the will on principles of reason in themselves; the second, dependence on principles of reason for the sake of inclination, reason supplying only the practical rules how the requirement of the inclination may be satisfied. In the first case the action interests me; in the second the object of the action (because it is pleasant to me). We have seen in the first section that in an action done from duty we must look not to the interest in the object, but only to that in the action itself, and in its rational principle (viz. the law).

tains besides the law only the necessity that the maxims[2] shall conform to this law, while the law contains no conditions restricting it, there remains nothing but the general statement that the maxim of the action should conform to a universal law, and it is this conformity alone that the imperative properly represents as necessary.

There is therefore but one categorical imperative, namely, this: *Act only on that maxim whereby thou canst at the same time will that it should become a universal law.*

Now if all imperatives of duty can be deduced from this one imperative as from their principle, then, although it should remain undecided whether what is called duty is not merely a vain notion, yet at least we shall be able to show what we understand by it and what this notion means.

Since the universality of the law according to which effects are produced constitutes what is properly called *nature* in the most general sense (as to form), that is the existence of things so far as it is determined by general laws, the imperative of duty may be expressed thus: *Act as if the maxim of thy action were to become by thy will a universal law of nature.*

We will now enumerate a few duties, adopting the usual division of them into duties to ourselves and to others, and into perfect and imperfect duties.[3]

1. A man reduced to despair by a series of misfortunes feels wearied of life, but is still so far in possession of his reason that he can ask himself whether it would not be contrary to his duty to himself to take his own life. Now he inquires whether the maxim of his action could become a universal law of

---

[2]A maxim is a subjective principle of action, and must be distinguished from the *objective principle*, namely, practical law. The former contains the practical rule set by reason according to the conditions of the subject (often its ignorance or its inclinations), so that it is the principle on which the subject *acts*; but the law is the objective principle valid for every rational being, and is the principle on which it *ought to act* that is an imperative.

[3]It must be noted here that I reserve the division of duties for a future *metaphysic of morals*; so that I give it here only as an arbitrary one (in order to arrange my examples). For the rest, I understand by a perfect duty one that admits no exception in favour of inclination, and then I have not merely external but also internal perfect duties. This is contrary to the use of the word adopted in the schools; but I do not intend to justify it here, as it is all one for my purpose whether it is admitted or not.

nature. His maxim is: From self-love I adopt it as a principle
to shorten my life when its longer duration is likely to bring
more evil than satisfaction. It is asked then simply whether
this principle founded on self-love can become a universal law
of nature. Now we see at once that a system of nature of which
it should be a law to destroy life by means of the very feeling
whose special nature it is to impel to the improvement of life
would contradict itself, and therefore could not exist as a
system of nature; hence that maxim cannot possibly exist as a
universal law of nature, and consequently would be wholly inconsistent with the supreme principle of all duty.

   2. Another finds himself forced by necessity to borrow
money. He knows that he will not be able to repay it, but
sees also that nothing will be lent to him, unless he promises
stoutly to repay it in a definite time. He desires to make
this promise, but he has still so much conscience as to ask
himself: Is it not unlawful and inconsistent with duty to get
out of a difficulty in this way? Suppose, however, that he re-
solves to do so, then the maxim of his action would be expressed thus: When I think myself in want of money, I will borrow money and promise to repay it, although I know that I never
can do so. Now this principle of self-love or of one's own advantage may perhaps be consistent with my whole future welfare;
but the question now is, Is it right? I change then the suggestion of self-love into a universal law, and state the question thus: How would it be if my maxim were a universal law?
Then I see at once that it could never hold as a universal law
of nature, but would necessarily contradict itself. For supposing it to be a universal law that everyone when he thinks
himself in a difficulty should be able to promise whatever he
pleases, with the purpose of not keeping his promise, the promise itself would become impossible, as well as the end that one
might have in view in it, since no one would consider that anything was promised to him, but would ridicule all such statements as vain pretences.

   3. A third finds in himself a talent which with the help
of some culture might make him a useful man in many respects.
But he finds himself in comfortable circumstances, and prefers
to indulge in pleasure rather than to take pains in enlarging
and improving his happy natural capacities. He asks, however,
whether his maxim of neglect of his natural gifts, besides
agreeing with his inclination to indulgence, agrees also with
what is called duty. He sees then that a system of nature
could indeed subsist with such a universal law although men
(like the South Sea islanders) should let their talents rest,
and resolve to devote their lives merely to idleness, amusement,
and propagation of their species—in a word, to enjoyment; but
he cannot possibly *will* that this should be a universal law of
nature, or be implanted in us as such by a natural instinct.

For, as a rational being, he necessarily wills that his faculties be developed, since they serve him, and have been given
him, for all sorts of possible purposes.

4. A fourth, who is in prosperity, while he sees that
others have to contend with great wretchedness and that he
could help them, thinks: What concern is it of mine? Let every
one be as happy as Heaven pleases, or as he can make himself;
I will take nothing from him nor even envy him, only I do not
wish to contribute anything to his welfare or to his assistance
in distress! Now no doubt if such a mode of thinking were a
universal law, the human race might very well subsist, and
doubtless even better than in a state in which everyone talks
of sympathy and good-will, or even takes care occasionally to
put it into practice, but, on the other side, also cheats when
he can, betrays the rights of men, or otherwise violates them.
But although it is possible that a universal law of nature
might exist in accordance with that maxim, it is impossible to
will that such a principle should have the universal validity
of a law of nature. For a will which resolved this would contradict itself, inasmuch as many cases might occur in which
one would have need of the love and sympathy of others, and in
which, by such a law of nature, sprung from his own will, he
would deprive himself of all hope of the aid he desires.

These are a few of the many actual duties, or at least
what we regard as such, which obviously fall into two classes
on the one principle that we have laid down. We must be *able
to will* that a maxim of our action should be a universal law.
This is the canon of the moral appreciation of the action generally. Some actions are of such a character that their maxim
cannot without contradiction be even *conceived* as a universal
law of nature, far from it being possible that we should *will*
that it *should* be so. In others this intrinsic impossibility
is not found, but still it is impossible to *will* that their
maxim should be raised to the universality of a law of nature,
since such a will would contradict itself. It is easily seen
that the former violate strict or rigorous (inflexible) duty;
the latter only laxer (meritorious) duty. Thus it has been
completely shown by these examples how all duties depend as regards the nature of the obligation (not the object of the action) on the same principle.

If now we attend to ourselves on occasion of any transgression of duty, we shall find that we in fact do not will
that our maxim should be a universal law, for that is impossible for us; on the contrary, we will that the opposite should
remain a universal law, only we assume the liberty of making an
exception in our own favour or (just for this time only) in
favour of our inclination. Consequently if we considered all
cases from one and the same point of view, namely, that of
reason, we should find a contradiction in our own will, namely,

that a certain principle should be objectively necessary as a universal law, and yet subjectively should not be universal, but admit of exceptions. As, however, we at one moment regard our action from the point of view of a will wholly conformed to reason, and then again look at the same action from the point of view of a will affected by inclination, there is not really any contradiction, but an antagonism of inclination to the precept of reason, whereby the universality of the principle is changed into a mere generality, so that the practical principle of reason shall meet the maxim half way. Now, although this cannot be justified in our own impartial judgment, yet it proves that we do really recognize the validity of the categorical imperative and (with all respect for it) only allow ourselves a few exceptions, which we think unimportant and forced from us. . . .

SELF-LOVE AND RESPECT FOR THE MORAL LAW

The direct opposite of the principle of morality is, when the principle of *private* happiness is made the determining principle of the will, and with this is to be reckoned, as I have shown above, everything that places the determining principle which is to serve as a law anywhere but in the legislative form of the maxim. This contradiction, however, is not merely logical, like that which would arise between rules empirically conditioned, if they were raised to the rank of necessary principles of cognition, but is practical, and would ruin morality altogether were not the voice of reason in reference to the will so clear, so irrepressible, so distinctly audible even to the commonest men. It can only, indeed, be maintained in the perplexing speculations of the schools, which are bold enough to shut their ears against that heavenly voice, in order to support a theory that costs no trouble.

Suppose that an acquaintance whom you otherwise liked were to attempt to justify himself to you for having borne false witness, first by alleging the, in his view, sacred duty of consulting his own happiness; then by enumerating the advantages which he had gained thereby, pointing out the prudence he had shown in securing himself against detection, even by yourself, to whom he now reveals the secret only in order that he may be able to deny it at any time; and suppose he were then to affirm, in all seriousness, that he has fulfilled a true human duty; you would either laugh in his face, or shrink back from him with disgust; and yet, if a man has regulated his principles of action solely with a view to his own advantage, you would have nothing whatever to object against this mode of proceeding. Or suppose some one recommends you a man as steward, as a man to whom you can blindly trust all your affairs; and,

in order to inspire you with confidence, extols him as a prudent man who thoroughly understands his own interest, and is so
indefatigably active that he lets slip no opportunity of ad-
vancing it; lastly, lest you should be afraid of finding a vulgar selfishness in him, praises the good taste with which he
lives: not seeking his pleasure in money-making, or in coarse
wantonness, but in the enlargement of his knowledge, in instructive intercourse with a select circle, and even in reliev-
ing the needy; while as to the means (which, of course, derive
all their value from the end) he is not particular, and is
ready to use other people's money for the purpose, as if it
were his own, provided only he knows that he can do so safely
and without discovery; you would either believe that the
recommender was mocking you, or that he had lost his senses.
So sharply and clearly marked are the boundaries of morality
and self-love that even the commonest eye cannot fail to distinguish whether a thing belongs to the one or the other. The
few remarks that follow may appear superfluous where the truth
is so plain, but at least they may serve to give a little more
distinctness to the judgment of common sense. . . .

The maxim of self-love (prudence) only *advises*; the law of
morality *commands*. Now there is a great difference between
that which we are *advised* to do and that to which we are
obliged.

The commonest intelligence can easily and without hesita-
tion see what, on the principle of autonomy of the will, requires to be done; but on supposition of heteronomy of the will,
it is hard and requires knowledge of the world to see what is
to be done. That is to say, what *duty* is, is plain of itself
to everyone; but what is to bring true durable advantage, such
as will extend to the whole of one's existence, is always
veiled in impenetrable obscurity; and much prudence is required
to adapt the practical rule founded on it to the ends of life,
even tolerably, by making proper exceptions. But the moral law
commands the most punctual obedience from everyone; it must,
therefore, not be so difficult to judge what it requires to be
done, that the commonest unpractised understanding, even without worldly prudence, should fail to apply it rightly.

It is always in everyone's power to satisfy the categorical command of morality; whereas it is but seldom possible, and
by no means so to everyone, to satisfy the empirically conditioned precept of happiness, even with regard to a single purpose. The reason is, that in the former case there is question
only of the maxim, which must be genuine and pure; but in the
latter case there is question also of one's capacity and physical power to realize a desired object. A command that everyone
should try to make himself happy would be foolish, for one
never commands anyone to do what he of himself infallibly wishes to do. We must only command the means, or rather supply

them, since he cannot do everything that he wishes. But to
command morality under the name of duty is quite rational; for,
in the first place, not everyone is willing to obey its precepts if they oppose his inclinations; and as to the means of
obeying this law, these need not in this case be taught, for in
this respect whatever he wishes to do he can do.

He who has *lost* at play may be *vexed* at himself and his
folly; but if he is conscious of having *cheated* at play (although he has gained thereby), he must *despise* himself as soon
as he compares himself with the moral law. This must, therefore, be something different from the principle of private happiness. For a man must have a different criterion when he is
compelled to say to himself: I am a *worthless* fellow, though I
have filled my purse; and when he approves himself, and says:
I am a *prudent* man, for I have enriched my treasure.

Finally, there is something further in the idea of our
practical reason, which accompanies the transgression of a
moral law—namely, its *ill desert*. Now the notion of punishment, as such, cannot be united with that of becoming a par-
taker of happiness; for although he who inflicts the punishment may at the same time have the benevolent purpose of
directing this punishment to this end, yet it must first be
justified in itself as punishment, *i.e.* as mere harm, so that
if it stopped there, and the person punished could get no
glimpse of kindness hidden behind this harshness, he must yet
admit that justice was done him, and that his reward was perfectly suitable to his conduct. In every punishment, as such,
there must first be justice, and this constitutes the essence
of the notion. Benevolence may, indeed, be united with it, but
the man who has deserved punishment, has not the least reason
to reckon upon this. Punishment, then, is a physical evil,
which, though it be not connected with moral evil as a *natural*
consequence, ought to be connected with it as a consequence by
the principles of a moral legislation. Now, if every crime,
even without regarding the physical consequence with respect to
the actor, is in itself punishable, that is, forfeits happiness
(at least partially), it is obviously absurd to say that the
crime consisted just in this, that he has drawn punishment on
himself, thereby injuring his private happiness (which, on the
principle of self-love, must be the proper notion of all crime).
According to this view the punishment would be the reason for
calling anything a crime, and justice would, on the contrary,
consist in omitting all punishment, and even preventing that
which naturally follows; for, if this were done, there would no
longer be any evil in the action, since the harm which otherwise followed it, and on account of which alone the action was
called evil, would now be prevented. To look, however, on all
rewards and punishments as merely the machinery in the hand
of a higher power, which is to serve only to set rational

creatures striving after their final end (happiness), this is
to reduce the will to a mechanism destructive of freedom; this
is so evident that it need not detain us.

More refined, though equally false, is the theory of those
who suppose a certain special moral sense, which sense and not
reason determines the moral law, and in consequence of which
the consciousness of virtue is supposed to be directly connected with contentment and pleasure; that of vice, with mental
dissatisfaction and pain; thus reducing the whole to the desire
of private happiness. Without repeating what has been said
above, I will here only remark the fallacy they fall into. In
order to imagine the vicious man as tormented with mental dissatisfaction by the consciousness of his transgressions, they
must first represent him as in the main basis of his character,
at least in some degree, morally good; just as he who is
pleased with the consciousness of right conduct must be conceived as already virtuous. The notion of morality and duty
must, therefore, have preceded any regard to this satisfaction,
and cannot be derived from it. A man must first appreciate the
importance of what we call duty, the authority of the moral law,
and the immediate dignity which the following of it gives to
the person in his own eyes, in order to feel that satisfaction
in the consciousness of his conformity to it, and the bitter
remorse that accompanies the consciousness of its transgression.
It is, therefore, impossible to feel this satisfaction or dissatisfaction prior to the knowledge of obligation, or to make
it the basis of the latter. A man must be at least half honest
in order even to be able to form a conception of these feelings.
I do not deny that as the human will is, by virtue of liberty,
capable of being immediately determined by the moral law, so
frequent practice in accordance with this principle of determination can, at last, produce subjectively a feeling of satisfaction; on the contrary, it is a duty to establish and to cultivate this, which alone deserves to be called properly the
moral feeling; but the notion of duty cannot be derived from
it, else we should have to suppose a feeling for the law as
such, and thus make that an object of sensation which can only
be thought by the reason; and this, if it is not to be a flat
contradiction, would destroy all notion of duty, and put in its
place a mere mechanical play of refined inclinations sometimes
contending with the coarser. . . .

What is essential in the moral worth of actions is *that
the moral law should directly determine the will*. If the determination of the will takes place in conformity indeed to the
moral law, but only by means of a feeling, no matter of what
kind, which has to be presupposed in order that the law may be
sufficient to determine the will, and therefore not *for the
sake of the law*, then the action will possess *legality* but not
morality. Now, if we understand by *motive* [or *spring*] (*elater*

animi) the subjective ground of determination of the will of a
being whose reason does not necessarily conform to the objective law, by virtue of its own nature, then it will follow,
first, that no motives can be attributed to the Divine will,
and that the motives of the human will (as well as that of
every created rational being) can never be anything else than
the moral law, and consequently that the objective principle of
determination must always and alone be also the subjectively
sufficient determining principle of the action, if this is not
merely to fulfil the *letter* of the law, without containing its
spirit.[4]

Since, then, for the purpose of giving the moral law influence over the will, we must not seek for any other motives
that might enable us to dispense with the motive of the law itself, because that would produce mere hypocrisy, without con-
sistency; and it is even *dangerous* to allow other motives (for
instance, that of interest) even to co-operate *along with* the
moral law; hence nothing is left us but to determine carefully
in what way the moral law becomes a motive, and what effect
this has upon the faculty of desire. For as to the question
how a law can be directly and of itself a determining principle
of the will (which is the essence of morality), this is, for
human reason, an insoluble problem and identical with the question: how a free will is possible. Therefore what we have to
show *à priori* is, not why the moral law in itself supplies a
motive, but what effect it, as such, produces (or, more correctly speaking, must produce) on the mind.

The essential point in every determination of the will by
the moral law, is that being a free will it is determined simply by the moral law, not only without the co-operation of sensible impulses, but even to the rejection of all such, and to
the checking of all inclinations so far as they might be opposed to that law. So far, then, the effect of the moral law
as a motive is only negative, and this motive can be known *à
priori* to be such. For all inclination and every sensible impulse is founded on feeling, and the negative effect produced
on feeling (by the check on the inclinations) is itself feeling; consequently, we can see *à priori* that the moral law, as a
determining principle of the will, must by thwarting all our
inclinations produce a feeling which may be called pain; and in
this we have the first, perhaps the only, instance in which we
are able from *à priori* considerations to determine the relation
of a cognition (in this case of pure practical reason) to the
feeling of pleasure or displeasure. All the inclinations

---

[4]We may say of every action that conforms to the law, but is
not done for the sake of the law, that it is morally good in
the *letter*, not in the *spirit* (the intention).

together (which can be reduced to a tolerable system, in which case their satisfaction is called happiness) constitute *self-regard* (*solipsismus*). This is either the *self-love* that consists in an excessive *fondness* for oneself (*philautia*), or satisfaction with oneself (*arrogantia*). The former is called particularly *selfishness*; the latter *self-conceit*. Pure practical reason only *checks* selfishness, looking on it as natural and active in us even prior to the moral law, so far as to limit it to the condition of agreement with this law, and then it is called *rational self-love*. But self-conceit reason *strikes down* altogether, since all claims to self-esteem which precede agreement with the moral law are vain and unjustifiable, for the certainty of a state of mind that coincides with this law is the first condition of personal worth (as we shall presently show more clearly), and prior to this conformity any pretension to worth is false and unlawful. Now the propensity to self-esteem is one of the inclinations which the moral law checks, inasmuch as that esteem rests only on morality. Therefore the moral law breaks down self-conceit. But as this law is something positive in itself, namely, the form of an intellectual causality, that is, of freedom, it must be an object of respect; for by opposing the subjective antagonism of the inclinations it *weakens* self-conceit; and since it even *breaks down*, that is, humiliates this conceit, it is an object of the highest respect, and consequently is the foundation of a positive feeling which is not of empirical origin, but is known *à priori*. Therefore respect for the moral law is a feeling which is produced by an intellectual cause, and this feeling is the only one that we know quite *à priori*, and the necessity of which we can perceive.

In the preceding chapter we have seen that everything that presents itself as an object of the will prior to the moral law is by that law itself, which is the supreme-condition of practical reason, excluded from the determining principles of the will which we have called the unconditionally good; and that the mere practical form which consists in the adaptation of the maxims to universal legislation first determines what is good in itself and absolutely, and is the basis of the maxims of a pure will, which alone is good in every respect. However, we find that our nature as sensible beings is such that the matter of desire (objects of inclination, whether of hope or fear) first presents itself to us; and our pathologically affected self, although it is in its maxims quite unfit for universal legislation, yet, just as if it constituted our entire self, strives to put its pretensions forward first, and to have them acknowledged as the first and original. This propensity to make ourselves in the subjective determining principles of our choice serve as the objective determining principle of the will generally may be called *self-love*; and if this pretends to be legislative as an unconditional practical principle, it may be called *self-conceit*. Now the moral law, which alone is truly objective (namely, in every respect), entirely excludes the influence of self-love on the supreme practical principle, and indefinitely checks the self-conceit that prescribes the subjective conditions of the former as laws. Now whatever checks our self-conceit in our own judgment humiliates; therefore the moral law inevitably humbles every man when he compares with it the physical propensities of his nature. That, the idea of which as a *determining principle of our will* humbles us in our self-consciousness, awakes *respect* for itself, so far as it is itself positive, and a determining principle. Therefore the moral law is even subjectively a cause of respect. Now since everything that enters into self-love belongs to inclination, and all inclination rests on feelings, and consequently whatever checks all the feelings together in self-love has necessarily, by this very circumstance, an influence on feeling; hence we comprehend how it is possible to perceive *à priori* that the moral can produce an effect on feeling, in that it excludes the inclinations and the propensity to make them the supreme practical condition, *i.e.* self-love, from all participation in the supreme legislation. This effect is on one side merely *negative*, but on the other side, relatively to the restricting principle of pure practical reason, it is *positive*. No special kind of feeling need be assumed for this under the name of a practical or moral feeling as antecedent to the moral law, and serving as its foundation.

The negative effect on feeling (unpleasantness) is *pathological*, like every influence on feeling, and like every feeling generally. But as an effect of the consciousness of the moral law, and consequently in relation to a supersensible cause, namely, the subject of pure practical reason which is the supreme lawgiver, this feeling of a rational being affected by inclinations is called humiliation (intellectual self-depreciation); but with reference to the positive source of this humiliation, the law, it is respect for it. There is indeed no feeling for this law; but inasmuch as it removes the resistance out of the way, this removal of an obstacle is, in the judgment of reason, esteemed equivalent to a positive help to its causality. Therefore this feeling may also be called a feeling of respect for the moral law, and for both reasons together *a moral feeling*.

While the moral law, therefore, is a formal determining principle of action by practical pure reason, and is moreover a material though only objective determining principle of the objects of action as called good and evil, it is also a subjective determining principle, that is, a motive to this action, inasmuch as it has influence on the morality of the subject, and produces a feeling conducive to the influence of the law on the will. There is here in the subject no *antecedent* feeling

tending to morality. For this is impossible, since every feeling is sensible, and the motive of moral intention must be free
from all sensible conditions. On the contrary, while the sensible feeling which is at the bottom of all our inclinations is
the condition of that impression which we call respect, the
cause that determines it lies in the pure practical reason; and
this impression therefore, on account of its origin, must be
called, not a pathological but a *practical effect*. For by the
fact that the conception of the moral law deprives self-love of
its influence, and self-conceit of its illusion, it lessens the
obstacle to pure practical reason, and produces the conception
of the superiority of its objective law to the impulses of the
sensibility; and thus, by removing the counterpoise, it gives
relatively greater weight to the law in the judgment of reason
(in the case of a will affected by the aforesaid impulses).
Thus the respect for the law is not a motive to morality, but
is morality itself subjectively considered as a motive, inasmuch as pure practical reason, by rejecting all the rival pretensions of self-love, gives authority to the law which now
alone has influence. Now it is to be observed that as respect
is an effect on feeling, and therefore on the sensibility, of
a rational being, it presupposes this sensibility, and therefore also the finiteness of such beings on whom the moral law
imposes respect; and that respect for the *law* cannot be attributed to a supreme being, or to any being free from all sensibility, in whom, therefore, this sensibility cannot be an
obstacle to practical reason.

This feeling [sentiment] (which we call the moral feeling)
is therefore produced simply by reason. It does not serve for
the estimation of actions nor for the foundation of the objective moral law itself, but merely as a motive to make this of
itself a maxim. But what name could we more suitably apply to
this singular feeling which cannot be compared to any pathological feeling? It is of such a peculiar kind that it seems
to be at the disposal of reason only, and that pure practical
reason. . . .

It is a very beautiful thing to do good to men from love
to them and from sympathetic good will, or to be just from love
of order; but this is not yet the true moral maxim of our conduct which is suitable to our position amongst rational beings
as *men* when we pretend with fanciful pride to set ourselves
above the thought of duty, like volunteers, and, as if we were
independent on the command, to want to do of our own good
pleasure what we think we need no command to do. We stand
under a *discipline* of reason, and in all our maxims must not
forget our subjection to it, nor withdraw anything therefrom,
or by an egotistic presumption diminish aught of the authority
of the law (although our own reason gives it) so as to set the
determining principle of our will, even though the law be

conformed to, anywhere else but in the law itself and in respect for this law. Duty and obligation are the only names
that we must give to our relation to the moral law. We are indeed legislative members of a moral kingdom rendered possible
by freedom, and presented to us by reason as an object of respect; but yet we are subjects in it, not the sovereign, and to
mistake our inferior position as creatures, and presumptuously
to reject the authority of the moral law, is already to revolt
from it in spirit, even though the letter of it is fulfilled.

   With this agrees very well the possibility of such a command as: *Love God above everything, and thy neighbour as thyself.*[5] For as a command it requires respect for a law which
commands love and does not leave it to our own arbitrary choice
to make this our principle. Love to God, however, considered
as an inclination (pathological love), is impossible, for he is
not an object of the senses. The same affection towards men is
possible no doubt, but cannot be commanded, for it is not in
the power of any man to love anyone at command; therefore it is
only *practical love* that is meant in that pith of all laws. To
love God means, in this sense, to like to do His commandments;
to love one's neighbour means to like to practise all duties
towards him. But the command that makes this a rule cannot
command us to *have* this disposition in actions conformed to
duty, but only to *endeavour* after it. For a command to like to
do a thing is in itself contradictory, because if we already
know of ourselves what we are bound to do, and if further we
are conscious of liking to do it, a command would be quite
needless; and if we do it not willingly, but only out of respect for the law, a command that makes this respect the motive
of our maxim would directly counteract the disposition commanded. That law of all laws, therefore, like all the moral precepts of the Gospel, exhibits the moral disposition in all its
perfection, in which, viewed as an Ideal of holiness, it is not
attainable by any creature, but yet is the pattern which we
should strive to approach, and in an uninterrupted but infinite
progress become like to. In fact, if a rational creature could
ever reach this point, that he thoroughly *likes* to do all moral
laws, this would mean that there does not exist in him even the
possibility of a desire that would tempt him to deviate from
them; for to overcome such a desire always costs the subject
some sacrifice, and therefore requires self-compulsion, that is,
inward constraint to something that one does not quite like to
do; and no creature can ever reach this stage of moral disposition. . . .

---

[5]This law is in striking contrast with the principle of private
happiness which some make the supreme principle of morality.
This would be expressed thus: *Love thyself above everything,
and God and thy neighbour for thine own sake.*

THE DUTY OF LOVE TOWARD OTHER MEN

. . . By a tendency of his nature man inevitably wants and seeks his own happiness, *i.e.* contentment with his state along with the assurance that it will last; and for this reason one's own happiness is not an obligatory end. —Some people, however, invent a distinction between moral happiness, which they define as contentment with our own person and moral conduct and so with what we *do*, and natural happiness, which is satisfaction with what nature bestows and so with what we *enjoy* as a gift from without. (I refrain here from censuring a misuse of the word "happiness" which already involves a contradiction.) It must therefore be noted that the feeling of moral happiness belongs only under the preceding heading of perfection; for the man who is said to be happy in the mere consciousness of his integrity already possesses the perfection defined there as the end which it is also his duty to have.

When it comes to my pursuit of happiness as an obligatory end, this must therefore be the happiness of *other* men, *whose* (permissible) *ends I thus make my own ends as well*. It is for them to decide what things they consider elements in their happiness; but I am entitled to refuse some of these things if I disagree with their judgments, so long as the other has no right to demand a thing from me as his due. But time and again an alleged *obligation* to attend to *my own* (natural) happiness is set up in competition with this end, and my natural and merely subjective end is thus made a duty (an obligatory end). . . . .

Our *well-wishing* can be unlimited, since in it we need do nothing. But *doing good* to others is harder, especially if we should do it from duty, at the cost of sacrificing and mortifying many of our desires, rather than from inclination (love) toward others. —The proof that beneficence is a duty follows from the fact that our self-love cannot be divorced from our need of being loved by others (*i.e.* of receiving help from them when we are in need), so that we make ourselves an end for others. Now our maxim cannot be obligatory [for others] unless it qualifies as a universal law and so contains the will to make other men our ends too. The happiness of others is, therefore, an end which is also a duty.

[The law says] only that I should sacrifice a part of my well-being to others without hope of requital, because this is a duty; it cannot assign determinate limits to the extent of this sacrifice. These limits will depend, in large part, on what a person's true needs consist of in view of his temperament, and it must be left to each to decide this for himself. For a maxim of promoting another's happiness at the sacrifice of my own happiness, my true needs, would contradict itself were it made a universal law. . . .

Love is a matter of *feeling*, not of *will*, and I cannot love because I *will* to, still less because I *ought* to (*i.e.* I cannot be necessitated to love). So a *duty to love* is logically impossible. But *benevolence* (*amor benevolentiae*), as conduct, can be brought under a law of duty. We often call unselfish benevolence to men *love* also (though this is most inappropriate); indeed we speak of love which is also our duty when it is not a question of another's happiness but of the complete and free surrender of all one's ends to the ends of another (even a supernatural) being. But every duty implies *necessitation* or constraint, even if the constraint is to be self-imposed according to a law. And what is done from constraint is not done from love.

To *help* other men according to our ability is a duty, whether we love them or not; and even if it turns out that the human species, on closer acquaintance, does not seem particularly lovable, this would not detract from the force of our duty to help others. —*Hatred of man* is always *hateful*, even if it takes the form merely of a complete withdrawal from men (separatist misanthropy), without active hostility toward them. For benevolence, even toward the misanthropist, remains always a duty, we cannot, indeed, love him, but we can still render good to him.

But to hate vice in men is neither a duty nor contrary to duty; it is rather a mere feeling of aversion from vice, a feeling neither influenced by the will nor exerting influence on the will. *Helping* others to achieve their ends is a duty. If a man practices it often and succeeds in realizing his purpose, he eventually comes to feel love for those he has helped. Hence the saying: you *ought* to *love* your neighbour as yourself, does not mean: you should immediately (first) love him and (afterwards) through the medium of this love do good to him. It means, rather: *do good* to your fellow-man, and this will give rise to love of man in you (as an aptitude of the inclination to beneficence in general). Hence only the love that is mere affection (*amor complacentiae*) is direct. But a duty to this kind of love (which is a pleasure joined immediately with the thought of an object's existence) is a contradiction, since one would have to be necessitated to take pleasure in the object. . . .

The first division of duties of virtue to others can be the division into duties by fulfilling which we also obligate the other, and duties whose observance does not result in obligation on the other's part. —To fulfill the first is *meritorious* (in relation to the other person); but to fulfill the second is to render the other only what is *due* to him. —*Love* and *respect* are the feelings that accompany the practice of these duties. They can be considered separately (each by itself) and can also exist separately (we can *love* our neighbour though he might deserve but little respect, and we can show him the *respect* necessary for every man though we might not think him very lovable). But in their ground in the law love and respect are always joined together in a duty, only in such a way that now one duty and now the other is the subject's principle, with the other joined to it as an accessory. —Thus we shall recognize an obligation to help a poor man; but since our favour humbles him by making his welfare dependent on our generosity, it is our duty to behave as if our help is either what is merely due to him or but a slight service of love, and so to spare him humiliation and maintain his self-respect.

When we are speaking of laws of duty (not laws of nature) and, among these, of laws governing men's external relations with one another, we are considering a moral (intelligible) world where, by analogy with the physical word, *attraction* and *repulsion* bind together rational beings (on earth). The principle of *mutual love* admonishes men constantly to *come nearer* to each other; that of the *respect* which they owe each other, to keep themselves at a *distance* from one another. And should one of these great moral forces fail, "then nothingness (immorality), with gaping throat, would drink the whole kingdom of (moral) beings like a drop of water" (if I may use Haller's words, but in a different connection).

In this context, however, *love* is not to be taken as a *feeling* (aesthetic love), *i.e.* a pleasure in the perfection of other men; it does not mean *emotional* love (for others cannot oblige us to have feelings). It must rather be taken as a maxim of *benevolence* (practical love), which has beneficence as its consequence.

The same holds true of the *respect* to be shown to others: it is not to be taken merely as the *feeling* that comes from comparing one's own *worth* with another's (such as mere habit causes a child to feel toward his parents, a pupil toward his teacher, a subordinate in general toward his superior). Respect is rather to be taken in a practical sense (*observantia aliis praestanda*), as a *maxim* of limiting our self-esteem by the dignity of humanity in another person.

Moreover, the duty of free respect to others is really only a negative one (of not exalting oneself above others) and is thus analogous to the juridical duty of not encroaching on another's possessions. Hence, although respect is a mere duty of virtue, it is considered *narrow* in comparison with a duty of love, and it is the duty of love that is considered *wide*.

The duty of love for one's neighbour can also be expressed as the duty of making others' *ends* my own (in so far as these ends are only not immoral). The duty of respect for my neighbour is contained in the maxim of not abasing any other man to a mere means to my end (not demanding that the other degrade himself in order to slave for my end).

By the fact that I fulfill a duty of love to someone I obligate the other as well: I make him indebted to me. But in fulfilling a duty of respect I obligate only myself, contain myself within certain limits in order to detract nothing from the worth that the other, as a man, is entitled to posit in himself.

Since we are now conceiving love of man (philanthropy) as practical, not emotional, love, we must locate it in active benevolence so that it has to do with the maxims of actions. —A man who finds satisfaction in the well-being (*salus*) of men simply as men and is glad when things go well for them is called a *friend of man* (philanthropist) in general. A man who is pleased only when things go ill with others is called an *enemy of man* (a misanthropist in the practical sense). A man who is indifferent to the welfare of others if only things go well for himself is a *self-seeker* (*solipsista*). —But a man who avoids other men because he can find no *pleasure* in them, though he indeed *wishes* them *well*, would be a *cynic* (an aesthetic misanthropist), and his aversion from men could be called anthropophobia.

According to the ethical law of perfection "love your neighbour as yourself," every man has a duty to others of adopting the maxim of benevolence (practical love of man), whether or not he finds them lovable. —For every morally-practical relation to men is a relation of men in the thought of pure reason, *i.e.* a relation of free actions according to maxims which qualify for giving universal law and which, therefore, cannot be self-seeking (*ex solipsismo prodeuntes*). I want every other man to be benevolent to me (*benevolentiam*); hence I should also be benevolent to every other man. But since all *other* men with the exception of myself would not be *all* men, and the maxim would then not have the universality of a law, as it must have in order to be obligatory, the law prescribing the duty of benevolence will include myself, as the object of benevolence, in the command of practical reason. —Not that I am thereby obligated to love myself (for this happens inevitably, apart from any command, and so there is no obligation to it); it is rather that legislative reason, which includes the whole species (and so myself with it) in its Idea of humanity as such (not of men), includes me, when it gives universal law, in the duty of mutual benevolence, according to the principle that I am equal with all others besides me, and *permits* you to be benevolent to *yourself* under the condition of your being benevolent to every other man as well. For it is only in this way that your maxim (of benevolence) qualifies for giving universal law—the principle on which every law of duty is based.

Now the benevolence present in the love of all men as such is indeed the greatest in its *extent*, but the smallest in its *degree*; and when I say: I take an interest in this man's wel-

fare only in keeping with my universal love for man, the interest I take in him is as slight as an interest can be. I am
only not indifferent with regard to him.

Yet one man is closer to me than another, and in benevolence I am the closest to myself. Now how does this fit with
the precept "love your *neighbour* (your fellowman) as yourself"?
When (in the duty of benevolence) one man is closer to me than
another, I am obligated to greater benevolence to him than to
the other; but I am admittedly closer to myself (even according
to duty) than any other. So it would seem that I cannot, without contradicting myself, say that I ought to love every man as
myself; for the standard of self-love would allow of no difference in degree. —But it is quite obvious that what is meant,
in this case, is not a mere benevolence in *wishes*, which is
really only a satisfaction in the well-being of all others and
does not even require me to contribute to their well-being
(every man for himself: God for us all). It refers, rather, to
active, practical benevolence (beneficence), which consists in
making another's well-being and happiness my *end*. For in wish-
ing I can be *equally* benevolent to everyone, whereas in acting
I can, without violating the universality of my maxim, vary the
degree greatly according to the different objects of my love
(one of whom concerns me more closely than the other).

To provide oneself with such comforts as are necessary
merely to enjoy life (to take care of one's body, but not to
the point of effeminacy) is a duty to oneself. The contrary of
this is to deprive oneself of the essential pleasures of life,
whether from avarice (of the slavish kind) or from exaggerated
(fanatical) discipline of one's natural inclinations. Both of
these are opposed to man's duty to himself.

But how can it be required, as a duty, that we go beyond
benevolence in our wishes regarding others (which costs us
nothing) and make this benevolence practical, so that everyone
who has the means should be *beneficent* to the needy? —Benevolence is satisfaction in another's happiness (well-being); but
beneficence is the maxim of making another's happiness one's
end, and the duty of beneficence is the necessitation that reason exercises on the agent to adopt this maxim as universal law.

It is not self-evident that any such law is to be found in
reason; on the contrary, the maxim "Every man for himself: God
(fortune) for us all" seems to be the most natural one.

It is every man's duty to be beneficent—that is, to promote, according to his means, the happiness of others who are
in need, and this without hope of gaining anything by it.

For every man who finds himself in need wishes to be
helped by other men. But if he lets his maxim of not willing
to help others in turn when they are in need become public, *i.e.*
makes this a universal permissive law, then everyone would likewise deny him assistance when he needs it, or at least would be

entitled to. Hence the maxim of self-interest contradicts itself when it is made universal law—that is, it is contrary to
duty. Consequently the maxim of common interest—of beneficence toward the needy—is a universal duty of men, and indeed
for this reason: that men are to be considered fellow-men—that
is, rational beings with needs, united by nature in one dwell-
ing place for the purpose of helping one another.

The *rich* man (the man supplied abundantly with means for
the happiness of others—that is, beyond his own needs) should
hardly every regard his beneficence as meritorious duty, even
though in practicing it he does put others under obligation.
The satisfaction he derives from his beneficence, which costs
him no sacrifice, is a kind of revelling in moral feelings.
—He must also carefully avoid any appearance of intending to
put the other under obligation, for if he showed such an intention (thereby humbling the other in his own eyes) he would not
be extending true beneficence. Rather, he must make it felt
that he is himself obliged by the other's acceptance or hon-
oured by it, hence that the duty is merely something that he
owes. But it is still better if he can practice his beneficence in complete secrecy. —This virtue is greater when the
benefactor's means are limited and he is strong enough quietly
to take on himself the hardship he spares the other. Then he
can really be considered morally *rich*.

How far should we expend our means in practicing beneficence? Surely not to the extent that we ourselves would finally come to need the charity of others. How much worth has beneficence extended with a cold hand (by a will to be put into
effect at one's death)? —What of the man who deprives another
of his *freedom* but, in exercising over him the supreme authority permitted by the law of the land, does so according to his
own idea of how to make that person happy (of how to do good to
his bondsman)? Can this man consider himself beneficent for
taking paternal care of his bondsman in keeping with *his own*
concept of happiness? Or is not the injustice of depriving
someone of his freedom a thing so opposed to juridical duty as
such that the man who freely consents to submit to this condition, counting on his master's beneficence, commits the supreme
rejection of his own humanity, and the master's utmost concern
for this man would not really be beneficence at all? Or could
the service which the master renders him be so great as to out-
weigh man's right? —I cannot do good to anyone according to
my concept of happiness (except to young children and the in-
sane), but only according to that of the one I intend to benefit; and I am not really being kind to someone if I force a
gift on him.

The ability to practice beneficence, which depends on
property, follows largely from the injustice of the government,
which favours certain men and so introduces an inequality of

wealth that makes others need help. This being the case, does the rich man's help to the needy, on which he so readily prides himself as something meritorious, really deserve to be called beneficence at all?

Gratitude consists in *honoring* a person because of a kindness he has done us. The feeling connected with this recognition is respect for the benefactor (who puts one under obligation). But the benefactor is viewed as only in relation of love to the one who receives his favour. —Even a mere heartfelt *benevolence* on another's part, without material results, deserves to be called a duty of virtue; and this is the basis for the distinction between *active* gratitude and the gratitude of mere *affection*.

Gratitude is a duty. It is not a mere *prudential* maxim of encouraging another to show me further beneficence by attesting my indebtedness to him for a past kindness (*gratiarum actio est ad plus dandum invitatio*); for in such a maxim I use him merely as a means to my further purposes. Gratitude is, rather, immediate necessitation by the moral law, *i.e.* duty.

But gratitude must also be considered, more especially, a *holy* duty—that is, a duty such that its transgression (as a scandalous example) can destroy in principle the moral motive to beneficence. A moral object is holy if the obligation with regard to it cannot be discharged completely by any act in conformity with the obligation (so that no matter what he does, the person who is under obligation always remains under obligation). Any other duty is an *ordinary* duty. —But one cannot, by any requital of a kindness received, rid oneself of the obligation for this kindness, since one can never win away from the benefactor his *priority* of merit: the merit of having been the first in benevolence. —Even a mere heartfelt benevolence, apart from any such act (of beneficence), is already a ground of obligation to gratitude. A grateful attitude of this kind is called *appreciativeness*.

So far as the *extension* of this gratitude is concerned, it reaches not merely to our contemporaries but also to our ancestors, even to those we cannot identify with certainty. It is for this reason, too, that we think it improper not to defend the ancients, whom we can regard as our teachers, from all attacks, accusations, and disdain, in so far as this is possible. But it is foolish to attribute a pre-eminence in talents and good will to the ancients in preference to the moderns—as if the world were steadily declining, according to laws of nature, from its original perfection—and to despise everything new in comparison with antiquity.

But the *intension* of gratitude—that is, the degree of obligation to this virtue—is to be judged by how beneficial the favour was to the obligated subject and how unselfishly it was bestowed on him. The minimal degree is to do an *equal* service for the benefactor, if he can receive it (if he is still living) or, if he is dead, to render it to others. [The minimum of gratitude requires one] not to regard a kindness received as a burden one would gladly be rid of (since the person so favoured stands a step lower than his benefactor, and this wounds his pride), but to accept the occasion for gratitude as a moral kindness—that is, an opportunity given one to couple gratitude with love of man, to combine *sensitivity* to others' benevolence (attentiveness to the slightest degree of it in thinking about duty) with the *cordiality* of a benevolent attitude of will, and so to cultivate one's love of man.

Sympathetic joy and sorrow (*sympathia moralis*) are really sensuous feelings of a pleasure or pain (which should therefore be called aesthetic) at another's state of happiness or sadness (shared feeling, feeling participated in). Nature has already implanted in man the susceptibility for these feelings. But to use this as a means to promoting active and rational benevolence is still a particular, though only a conditioned, duty. It is called the duty of *humanity* (*humanitas*) because it regards man not merely as a rational being but also as an animal endowed with reason. Now humanity can be located either in the *power* and *will* to *share* in others' *feelings* (*humanitas practica*) or merely in the *susceptibility*, given by nature itself, to feel joy and sadness in common with others (*humanitas aesthetica*). The first is *free*, and for this reason it is called a *partaking* (*communio sentiendi liberalis*); it is based on practical reason. The second is *unfree* (*communio sentiendi illiberalis, servilis*); like the communication of warmth or contagious diseases it can be called an *imparting* and also a suffering with another, since it spreads by natural means among men living near one another. It is only to *humanitas practica* that there is an obligation.

The Stoic showed a noble cast of mind when he had his Sage say: I want a friend, not that he might help me in poverty, sickness, imprisonment, *etc.*, but rather that I might stand by him and rescue a man. But the same Sage, when he could not save his friend, said to himself: what is it to me? In other words, he repudiated imparted suffering.

When another person suffers and, although I cannot help him, I let myself be infected by his sorrow (by means of my imagination), then the two of us suffer, though the evil actually (in nature) affects only one. But there cannot possibly be a duty to increase the evil in the world, and so it cannot be a duty to do good from *sympathetic sadness*. This would also be an insulting kind of beneficence, since it expressed benevolence with regard to the unworthy, called *pity*, which has no place in men's relations with one another; for men are not allowed to boast about their worthiness to be happy.

But while it is not in itself a duty to experience sadness, and so also joy, in sympathy with others, it is a duty to participate actively in the fate of others. Hence we have an indirect duty to cultivate the sympathetic natural (aesthetic) feelings in us and to use them as so many means to participating from moral principles and from the feeling appropriate to these principles. —Thus it is our duty: not to avoid places where we shall find the poor who lack the most basic essentials, but rather to seek them out; not to shun sick-rooms or debtors' prisons in order to avoid the painful sympathetic feelings that we cannot guard against. For this is still one of the impulses which nature has implanted in us so that we may do what the thought of duty alone would not accomplish.

Would it not be better for the welfare of the world in general if human morality were limited to juridical duties and these were fulfilled with the utmost conscientiousness, while benevolence were considered morally indifferent? It is not so easy to see what effect this would have on man's happiness. But at least a great moral ornament, love of man, would then be missing from the world. Accordingly benevolence is required for its own sake, in order to present the world in its full perfection as a beautiful moral whole, even if we do not take into account the advantage it brings (in the way of happiness).

Gratitude is not properly mutual love for the benefactor by the man he has put under obligation, but rather *respect* for him. For universal love of one's neighbour can and must be based on equality of duty, whereas in gratitude the one obligated stands a step lower than his benefactor. Is it not this— namely pride—that causes so much ingratitude?—seeing another person above oneself and feeling repugnance at not being able to make oneself fully his equal (so far as relations of duty are concerned)? . . .

Moritz Schlick

HEDONISM AND EGOISM

From *Problems of Ethics*, by Moritz Schlick, translated by David Rynin (New York: Dover Publications, Inc., 1939, 1962). Reprinted through the permission of the publisher. Reprinted here are selections from chapters 2 and 3 (pp. 31-78); subheadings have been

omitted. Moritz Schlick (1882-1936) was professor of
philosophy of science at the University of Vienna and
was one of the chief organizers of the famed Vienna
Circle, a group of scientifically oriented philosophers
who considered mathematics and the physical sciences
to be the models of genuine knowledge and who rejected
traditional metaphysics as meaningless.

WHAT ARE THE MOTIVES OF HUMAN CONDUCT?

As we learn from experience, not every human action allows
of moral judgment; the greater part of our lives is filled with
activities which, considered in themselves, are beyond good and
evil. All our daily activities, work and play, necessities as
well as amusements, are formed of a vast number of complicated
movements which may be executed well or poorly, but which cannot be called "good" or "evil." How we place our feet when
walking, hold a pen when writing, or move our fingers in piano-
playing is, from the ethical point of view, perfectly indifferent. The exceptions in which activities of this sort are sub-
jected to moral judgment are easily shown to be merely apparent.
If, for example, a pianist pains his audience because of clumsy
finger movements, his errors are, under certain conditions,
morally disapproved; but closer examination shows that the
judgment refers not to the activity of the hands themselves,
but only to the prior resolution to appear before the public
with insufficient technique.

This holds in general. Ethics has to do only with "reso-
lutions." Certain acts against which the stream of activity
breaks stand out in the regular flow of activity that fills our
existence (and is morally irrelevant). These acts represent
the decisions of life; they alone deserve the name of "conduct";
all else is mere "activity."

How is conduct distinguished from mere activity? To begin
with, the personality is much more implicated in conduct; it
rises from greater depths, while activity is external, more
superficial, and often fails to come to the light of consciousness. But the difference must be more sharply drawn. Psychology offers us a means of doing this, since it applies to genuine conduct the significant title of "acts of will." In mere
activity no act of will or decision occurs. Such activity
occurs as immediate, although not necessarily unconscious, reactions to definite stimuli. In playing the piano the perception of written notes calls forth the corresponding finger
movement without any intervening act of will. The player does
not continuously decide, "Now I shall move this finger, now
that, and now my arm," and so forth. The action proceeds
according to the "ideo-motor" pattern, that is, an idea or a

perception or some sensation functions directly as a stimulus;
or, speaking psychologically, a stimulus of the sensory centers
of the nervous system flows directly into the motor centers and
brings forth the corresponding movement without delay.
   This is the normal course of all our acts. It would never
be disturbed, our whole life would run colorlessly on in mere
activity, and there would be no acts of will, if at any time
only *one* stimulus were at work. In such a case we would never
have formed the concept of "will," we would have had no occasion for, or possibility of, doing so. What we call an act of
will occurs only where several stimuli are at work simultaneously, to which one cannot respond at the same time, because
they lead to incompatible activities. What happens in such a
case of "conflicting motives?" In general, the following:
there occurs a peculiar oscillation of events of consciousness,
namely, a more or less rapid shift of ideas, which alternately
appear and disappear, as weaker and stronger, clearer and more
confused. They are the imaginative pictures of the results of
the different activities aroused by the stimuli, which in this
manner attempt, so to speak, to triumph over one another, dispute the possession of the field of attention, and mutually
inhibit one another.
   Let us consider a very simple case. I decide to leave
the room. I go to the door and press the latch. All this occurs automatically; the walking, the movement of my arm and
hand, proceed without any act of will being necessary. Now I
press the latch and pull on the door—but it does not open!
The usual course of events is disturbed. While hitherto, perhaps, I have been thinking of very different matters, now my
attention is centered upon the door. I shake it vigorously,
sense the tightening of my muscles, and experience exertion
against what opposes me. The idea of opening the door stands
firmly and clearly before me as an image of my goal. I "will"
to open the door.
   I believe that the specific experience of "willing" in the
whole affair is nothing but the "feeling of exertion" (whether
this is simply a feeling of tenseness in the muscles or some
special "innervation-sensation" does not concern us here). If
the door offers opposition for a long time, the question occurs
to me, shall I not desist, and wait until the perhaps inadvert-
ently closed door is opened, or shall I rather seek another
exit from the room? In this way the outer inhibition leads to
an inner one; the conflict between the end-in-view and the perceived state of affairs turns into a conflict between ideas,
between that of exit by force, and that of remaining, or of
leaving by the window. These ideas oppose each other; one will
triumph, and this triumph is obviously a "decision," an "act
of will."

In any act of will we find a struggle against an inner or
outer check, which ends with triumph or surrender. For ethics,
only the case of inner checks is of any importance; therefore
we restrict ourselves to the investigation of those acts of
will in which a definite idea (motive, or end-in-view) is in
conflict with another or several, and which finally dominates
it or them, that is, actually leads to overt activity. . . .

Be that as it may, the question which here concerns us as
philosophers is, "What determines whether a certain idea triumphs or succumbs in the conflict of motives? What properties
distinguish the prevailing motive?" Or, in a more appropriate
formulation, "Under what conditions does a definite idea gain
the upper hand?" The answer to this question tells us why a
man does this rather than that, why in general he prefers something, "wills" something. It is the answer to the question,
"What are the motives of human conduct?"

In many, indeed most, situations of life the answer is
easy to find; it lies so clearly at hand that it can be correctly given without further trouble by any unprejudiced judge,
that is, by any man not led astray by philosophizing and moral-
izing. Such a person will tell us that, at least in general,
in a conflict of several ends-in-view, a man will act in the
direction of the *most pleasant*.

What does this statement mean?

Every idea, every content of our consciousness, as we
learn from experience, possesses a certain *tone*. And this has
the consequence that the content in question is not something
completely neutral, or indifferent, but is somehow characterized as agreeable or disagreeable, attractive or repellent,
joyful or painful, pleasant or unpleasant. We adopt the last
mentioned terminology and say, every experience has an emotional tone that is pleasant or unpleasant, or, in the substantival
language of psychology, in every experience there is a feeling
of pleasure or of pain. The essence of these feelings is of
course indescribable—every simple experience is beyond all
description—and one can only make clear what is meant by appropriate indications. Here we should note that we use the
words "pleasant" and "unpleasant" in the widest possible sense.
All further questions, such as whether there are different
kinds of pleasantness and unpleasantness, or only different
grades, we put aside; most of them, like the one just mentioned,
seem to me to be improperly formulated. Of course, I have very
different experiences when I stroke soft silk, when I attend a
performance of *Midsummer Night's Dream*, when I admire an heroic
act, when the proximity of a beloved person makes me happy; but
in a certain respect there is undoubtedly a similarity in the
mental dispositions in all these cases, and we express this
when we say that all of them have *pleasant* emotional tones, or
that all of them are *joyful*. On the other hand, however differ-

ent my feelings may be when I cut my finger, when I hear a vio-
linist play a false note, when I think of the injustice of the
world, when I stand at the bier of a friend, there is some kind
of similarity in all these cases which still justifies me in
considering them all as belonging to a single class, and in saying they are *unpleasant* feelings.

The enumeration of these examples should not be misunder-
stood. In exceptional cases it may very well be that the last
mentioned situations are pleasant, and those mentioned first unpleasant. Sensations of bodily pain can be pleasant (perversion), false violin tones can amuse and please me (as in the
case of intended comedy), indeed, a pessimistic philosopher can
even be pleased with the injustice of the world, viewing it
triumphantly as a confirmation of his views: "I told you so!"
No definite emotional tone belongs to a specific experience as
such; it depends upon the whole situation, just as a white object can appear in any color, depending upon the lighting.

After these explanations we can state that the decision of
the will proceeds in the direction of the most pleasant end-in-
view, in the following manner: of the ideas which function as
motives, that one gains the upper hand which finally possesses
the highest degree of pleasant emotional tone, or the least unpleasant tone, and thus the act in question is unambiguously
determined. . . .

Having thus become clear regarding the *meaning* of the law,
that in the conflict of motives the decision goes to the most
pleasant or least unpleasant, we turn now to the question of
its *validity*.

I have already remarked that, for the majority of cases of
every-day acts of will, its validity is indisputable and obvious. When a child reaches for the largest of several cakes
offered it, when I take a walk in the open air instead of going
to a faculty meeting, when I reflect whether the destination of
a summer's trip shall be the sea or the mountains, when one
wavers between a visit to the opera or to a concert, between
buying black or brown shoes—then, normally, in all these cases
and in a thousand similar ones, there is not the shadow of a
doubt that the decision is determined by the agreeableness or
disagreeableness, by the pleasure quality of the end-in-view,
and that it takes place in the described way.

But in order to pursue the study of ethics, indeed to
understand the mechanism of conduct at all, we are little
served by a rule that holds good in the majority of cases only;
we need a *law*, that is, a description of relationships that
fits *all* cases. Now the familiar method always used by science
is to ask whether a rule verified in many cases may not itself
be a law, that is, actually hold for *all* cases. At any rate,
one begins with this assumption and often finds it verified, in
that all cases which at first sight seem not to fit the rule

are apparent exceptions only, their actual subsumption under the law being hidden by complicated circumstances.

Applying this method to our problem, we express the provisional assumption that the rule governing many cases of motivation may itself be a law, that is, we examine whether or not in *every* case of an act of will the decision be not determined in the direction of the most pleasant, or least unpleasant, motive.

At first sight this seems not to be the case at all. It happens that a well-bred child chooses the smallest cake, even though it obviously would "rather have" the largest; and do we not very often find ourselves in the situation of the child and trudge toward a painful, unpleasant goal? Does this not happen whenever we "make a sacrifice?" The fact is, many, if not most, philosophers believe that in such situations the prevailing motive is certainly not the most pleasant, and is often extremely unpleasant. Therefore, they do not consider the law to be universally valid; they deny it represents the law of motivation, and say it is not at all true that a man can desire only that the idea of which possesses relatively greater pleasure for him. They hold that he can desire simply anything, and many of them (including Kant) are of the opinion that although human conduct is determined by pleasant or unpleasant feelings in the described manner in all other cases, this is simply not so in the case of *moral acts*. The latter, according to them, form an exception and are, indeed, defined and distinguished by this fact. Hence we see the extent and importance of our problem, and we cannot be content before learning whether our law of motivation holds only in the limited sphere of the trivial acts of every-day life, or whether it is a true law governing every act of will without exception.

Let us not hesitate to analyze more closely the case of the child who has to choose between its several cakes. If the child takes the smallest in order to leave the larger ones for its companions, one may well consider this to be a "moral" act. Can its behavior really not be explained in terms of the law that the most pleasant end-in-view determines the will? I believe that we must admit that this is very easily done. For how is the state of mind of this child distinguished from that of the other who thoughtlessly takes the largest? We said before that even the child who here decides to make a "sacrifice" would "rather have" a larger piece of cake than a smaller one. But what is the significance of this? Obviously, that under otherwise similar conditions the idea of the larger cake is more pleasant (in the sense previously defined) than is that of the smaller. But conditions here are not the same, since in the mind of the child who renounces, because of his education or natural propensities, certain events are happening which are absent in the other child; and these act so that the original emotional tone of the conflicting ends-in-view is entirely

altered. They are events of association by means of which
there enter, more or less clearly, into consciousness ideas of
pleased or displeased parents, their words of praise or censure,
or the ideas of happy or disappointed companions. The strong
emotional tones that belong to all these ideas are transmitted
to the motive with which they are associated, and completely
modify its initial pleasure value. The image of a larger piece
of cake is indeed more pleasant than that of a smaller one if
both stand side by side unaccompanied by other ideas, but here
each is joined by a complex of other ideas together with their
feelings, and these feelings are transferred, as experience
shows, to those images, even when the ideas to which they
originally belonged no longer appear in consciousness. By this
process the idea of the lesser good can easily become more
pleasant than that of the greater, and the apparently paradoxical decision occurs in complete conformity with our law of motivation. Every one admits that the act of will could take
place as it did only because of certain external influences,
for no one believes that a child can choose the smaller cake
merely because it likes the larger one more. And pedagogical
experience teaches us that these influences are of the sort
described. Since this suffices to explain the fact completely,
we need no further hypothesis. Thus our law of motivation has
here been entirely verified; and it is verified in all other
cases we may choose to consider. Having dealt with a very
simple example, we do well now to turn our attention to those
acts of will in which the very highest matters are at stake,
and which have from olden times been drawn into the foreground
of ethical inquiries. Such are the cases of seemingly-greatest
renunciation, or self-sacrifice.

The idea of personal destruction is, in general, one of
the most terrifying; not the most terrifying, for there are
enough miseries in comparison with which death is felt as a
soothing relief. Yet we observe, in life and history, acts of
will whose fatal and miserable consequences are not only inevitable for the performer, but are clearly seen by him to be
involved as the goal of his action. The martyr accepts pain
and death for the sake of an idea, a friend gives his life or
"happiness" for his friend. Can any one in earnest say of such
persons that their decisions are determined by the motives
which possess the most pleasant or the least unpleasant emotional tones?

According to my firm conviction, one cannot say anything
else if one would tell the truth, for such are the facts. Let
us then try to analyze and understand the motive of heroism.
The hero acts "for the sake of a cause"; he desires to carry
out an idea or realize a definite goal. It is clear that the
thought of this goal or that idea dominates his consciousness
to such an extent that there is in it hardly room for any other

thoughts. At least this holds in the case of inspiration, from
which alone an heroic act can arise. It is true that the idea
of his own painful destruction is present, but, however burdened with pain it may be in itself, it is inhibited and re-
pressed by the predominant end-in-view, which finally triumphs
in an "act of will," in an effort which becomes stronger and
sharper the longer and more clearly the thought of the unavoidable catastrophe confronts him. What is the source of the as-
tonishing force of the decisive end-in-view? Whence the power
of this affect? Without doubt this is due to *emotion*. Inspiration is the greatest pleasure that can fall to the lot of
man. To be inspired by something means to be overcome by the
greatest joy in the thought of it. The man who, under the
stress of inspiration, decides to help a friend or save another
creature from pain and destruction, whatever the cost, finds
the thought of this act so profoundly joyful, so overwhelmingly
pleasant that, at the moment, the idea of the preservation of
his own life and the avoidance of pain cannot compare with it.
And he who fights for a cause with such inspiration that he
accepts all persecution and insult realizes his idea with such
elevated pure joy that neither the thought of his miseries nor
their actual pain can prevail aught against it. The notion of
giving up his purpose because of pain is, for him, more unpleasant than the pain itself.

Thus the correctness of our law of the will is shown in
even the most extreme case, and quite naturally, without any
auxiliary hypothesis. It is, in fact, universally true that
the will follows the motive which has the greatest degree of
pleasant feeling connected with it.

It was, of course, a gross error to try, as men did on
the basis of a naïve psychology, to explain the action of the
martyr by saying that his behavior is determined by a hope of
reward in another world, beyond; in this fashion apparently
subsuming it under our law of the will. This explanation may
often fit, but certainly not always, for there have been un-
believing martyrs, concerned only with this world. Indeed, it
does not hold even in the majority of cases, even though Schil-
ler has the Maid of Orleans die with the words, "The pain is
brief, the joy is everlasting." [*"Kurz ist der Schmerz, und
ewig ist die Freude."*]

No, it is not at all necessary that the prevailing pleasant idea be of one's personal condition. Why should this be
assumed? Perhaps because one believes that, in general, only
ideas of one's own condition can be pleasant, or, at least,
that only such ideas can be intensely pleasant? This would be
a gross misunderstanding of the psychological fact, for the
commonest experiences teach us the opposite. They also teach
that a man is not nearly so much concerned with his own future
good and evil as many older ethical systems would have us be-

lieve. For example, one can easily see this in the way a man
harms himself by being immoderate. When he squanders his future happiness for a mess of pottage, why should he not risk it
for the sake of the joy given him in saving some unfortunate?

If we are not clear in this, we run the danger of estab-
lishing our law of motivation in an erroneous manner, and hence
missing its truth. In fact, such mistaken notions at this
point are to blame for the fact that many hold our law to be
false. They suppose it to be absurd to say that the martyr
suffers and dies because of "pleasure," since in this way one
seems to wipe out, either in fact or at least terminologically,
all difference between the pleasant and the unpleasant.

When it comes to the confusion of the facts I believe that
our representation has avoided just that to which our opponents
have fallen victim. It is not a confusion, but on the contrary
a finer distinction, if we emphasize that an ordinarily painful
experience can, under special conditions, become pleasant, and
vice versa. It is this fact that is overlooked by the opponents of our view when they say that a man can act in the direction of any end-in-view, and not only toward a pleasant one.
To be sure, any end can be desired, but this does not mean that
it has nothing to do with the pleasure tone of the end-in-view,
but only that any end can become pleasant. It is as if one
said, "Whoever is not blind can see any visible thing." Of
course, but only if it be illuminated!

The will can no more direct itself toward an end, the idea
of which is simply unpleasant and has absolutely nothing attractive, alluring, or noble in it, than the eye can see an object clothed in utter darkness. In ethical considerations we
often come upon the assertion that man can desire that which is
in every respect painful and unenjoyable to him; but all examples that can be offered of such a desire show upon analysis
that the end is imagined as in some way still something noble,
great, necessary, propitiative, or valued, no matter how much
woe may be connected with it. As soon as one succeeds (which
is not so easy) in imagining an end that appears to be *completely* unpleasant, repulsive, disgusting, bringing suffering,
and hateful without compensation, without any possibility of
transfiguration, exhaltation or admiration, then one sees at
once with complete certainty that such an end *cannot* be desired. It is an inescapable law that the absolutely repulsive
and unpleasant is not a possible object of desire. Martyrs are
of course often fanatics, and a fanatic often inclines toward
perversion; hence bodily pain can then be pleasant for him.
But this case is very rare, although it frequently happens that
the *idea* of an ordinarily painful state is a joyful one for him.

With this we arrive at a second factual distinction, which
is frequently neglected by those who deny our law of the will.
It is the distinction between the *pleasant idea of a state* and

the *idea of a pleasant state*. That is, one can imagine only a
thing, a state, or an event, but not the pleasure connected
with the things; whether the idea itself is joyful or painful
does not at all depend on whether the imagined things, when
they are actually present, have pleasant or unpleasant consequences. As is well known, Dante thought that there was no
greater pain than that connected with the idea of a pleasant
state—if this lay in the past, *Nessun maggior dolore* . . .
Our law is concerned only with whether an idea is pleasant, and
not with whether it is the idea of something pleasant.

Regarding the objection, often raised, that the law of motivation can be maintained only by a trick of terminology,
since one extends the concept of pleasure too widely and desig-
nates very different things by the one word, we must say that
the real reason for our usage, in grouping together everything
which is pleasant or satisfying, lies in the facts. The usage
is perfectly natural, and is subsequently justified because it
leads to a simple formulation of a fundamental law. And how
else would one define the concept of pleasure? The objection
raised above cannot be considered a serious one. Of course, we
could agree to call only the satisfaction of hunger, thirst,
and the sexual impulse "pleasure"—which, perhaps, certain mor-
alists would prefer—but in so doing we should merely satisfy
certain prejudices, and it would be necessary to give up the
adequate formulation of the law of motivation.

No serious danger, then, threatens our law from this
quarter; and one actually finds the conviction of its validity
very widespread. Even many philosophers who explicitly oppose
it, implicitly presuppose its validity. The institutions of
human society all show the universal belief in the validity of
the law. For no religion, no system of education, no public
institution knows any other means of influencing human action
than to strive to make the idea of the end whose realization is
desired as pleasant as possible, and the idea of the undesired
unpleasant. The clumsiest means of doing this is the promise
of reward and the threat of punishment, but there are also more
refined, indirect means. . . .

WHAT IS EGOISM?

Many philosophers have thought that a will determined in
the described manner, by the maximum pleasure, must be called
egoistic; because it is supposed to be egoistic, or selfish, to
"seek one's own pleasure." And this holds even of those thinkers, like Spinoza, who had a presentiment of the validity of
our law, as well as of those, such as Kant, who denied it. The
former merely desired to express a fact, but in so doing gave
to the word "egoism" so broad a meaning that it became quite

useless; the latter desired to discredit the law of the will.
They used the word "egoism" with the uncomplimentary meaning
which it has in everyday life; but they did not realize that
in *this* sense conduct is certainly not at all egoistic when
it occurs in accordance with our law of motivation. For no un-
biassed person will call an act egoistic which, for example,
arises out of joy in the satisfactions of another person.

There is no doubt that in everyday speech this word is
used with the intention of blaming; that is, when someone calls
certain conduct egoistic he desires to call up an unpleasant
idea of this conduct. Also there is no doubt that such condemnation is intended as *moral* condemnation: the word "egoistic"
signifies a concept subsumed under the concept of the "immoral."
Thus egoism is a subspecies of immorality. By learning what is
meant by egoism we learn in part what is meant by "immorality,"
and this gives us a clue to the meaning of "morality," its opposite. If those philosophers were right who hope to derive
all immorality from "egoism," and who see in it the source of
all evil, then with the discovery of the meaning of the word
the whole question of the nature of the moral would practically
be answered; for it would only be necessary to separate what is
indifferent (if anything of the sort exists) from what is not
egoistic to find the moral in the remainder.

But, however this may be, in any case the inquiry concerning the nature of egoism can only consist in determining the
sense in which the word is actually used. It cannot determine
that a certain kind of behavior is "really" egoism, and that
nothing else can bear this name.

The most convenient, easiest assertion that a philosopher
can make about egoism is that it is an "impulse." Thus we find
Schopenhauer saying that all human conduct can be explained by
the existence of three "main-springs" of conduct, namely, egoism, malice, and sympathy. This would be an extremely simple
mechanism, and further explanation of the three impulses does
appear at first very simple. Egoism (according to Schopenhauer
and many others) aims at "one's own welfare"; sympathy aims at
"another's welfare" and corresponds to altruism; and malice
aims at "harm to others." . Thus, according to this teaching,
one's own welfare and the welfare or harm of others constitute
the three situations possessing human interest. The "satisfaction" of an impulse would consist in the realization of its
corresponding situation. Is it not significant that in this
list there is no impulse directed toward "one's own harm?"

It is easy to see that in this manner it is impossible to
get a definition of egoism, or even to understand the nature of
an impulse in general. For one must know first what one's "own
welfare" is. Does it not consist in the fact that one's own
desires are fulfilled, that is, that one's impulses are satisfied? Consequently, if one is sympathetic, the other's welfare

means at the same time the realization of one's own desires; if a man is malicious he is satisfied in knowing the other to suffer, and thereby his own welfare is increased. In other words, an act springing out of malice or sympathy would be just as egoistic as conduct motivated by egoism.

We learn from this paradox that by "welfare" one cannot mean the realization of all personal desires, the satisfaction of all of one's own impulses, without giving up the definition of egoism as the impulse aiming at "personal welfare." One of the two at least must be given up. In fact, both must be abandoned in order to obtain a clear idea that will do justice to the actual use of the word. For if one tries to improve Schopenhauer's thought, retaining his way of looking at the matter, by saying that "welfare" means the realization of all desires *with the exception* of those arising from malice or sympathy, then we must ask: with what right are such different activities as striving for power, knowledge, sexual pleasure, enjoyment of an art considered to be expressions of *one* impulse, namely "egoism?" This cannot be justified by linguistic usage, for the desires directed, for example, toward knowledge or aesthetic enjoyment are not usually called egoistic; nor can it be grounded in the facts, for evidently we have here a large variety of different "impulses," and the word "egoism" would only be a collective name for them. It would not be coordinated with the impulses, but would stand, as it were, behind or over them, as an impulse of a higher order. Such an impulse, which aimed at the satisfaction of impulses, would of course be a meaningless notion; and thus we discover the extreme carelessness of the usual formulation of the concept, carelessness that makes it impossible to talk clearly and sensibly concerning this matter. . . .

Inevitably, then, we arrive at the conclusion that egoism is not an impulse, and that to this word corresponds a complicated meaning. This meaning is of great importance for ethics, and we must inquire into it further.

Following the preceding considerations, we need no longer pursue the possibility that "egoism," although not a single impulse, might mean a common property of a series of different impulses. For these considerations showed us that the mere striving for something, the fact that some idea awakens feelings of pleasure is not itself enough to constitute "selfishness." We cannot, for example, separate out a group of "sensual impulses" and call these egoistic. (This has often been tried, apparently in the hope of finding in sense-pleasure the readiest substitute for the difficult concept of "personal welfare.") In this connection one always thinks of hunger, thirst, and the sexual impulse. And in fact one cannot extend the concept of sensual desire much further without obtaining wholly indeterminate boundaries, since the senses play an important role in the other impulses, too, as in the aesthetic ones; and the distinction between "interested" and "disinterested" pleasure, as Kant wished to formulate it is, I think, incapable of being complete-ly carried out. Every man has these so-called sensual inclina-tions, and could not exist without them; but they do not make an egoist of him, not even in the moments when they determine his action. In eating, drinking and procreating a man is far from conducting himself egoistically.

Something altogether different is needed in addition. Selfishness is neither an impulse nor a collective name for a group of impulses. The satisfaction of an impulse is never in itself egoistic; but only the manner in which this occurs, only the circumstances in which it takes place can give rise to that fact which we wish to characterize by the disparaging word "egoism."

And thus we attain the important insight (perhaps first expressed in the ethics of Bishop Butler) that by the word "selfishness" a fairly complex fact is designated, namely, the existence of a certain relative strength between the inclina-tions. For when we charge someone with egoism we do not blame him for the presence of a certain impulse, as when we accuse him of envy or cruelty, but we condemn him because under the given conditions just this impulse led to action; we would have demanded the omission of this act, or the commission of another. However, he would have been able to act otherwise only if some other inclination had been present to repress the original im-pulse and direct volition toward another goal; but such oppos-ing inclinations were absent or too weak with respect to the first. Which are these impulses whose absence or weakness lead to selfish conduct? They are obviously the "social impulses." These are the impulses whose essence consists in the fact that the perception or imagination of modes of behavior or states of *fellow men* leads directly to feelings of pleasure or pain. One may well describe them as the *altruistic* impulses, but this will entail an asymmetry in the use of the words "egoism" and "altruism." A man in whom the altruistic inclinations are ab-sent has no immediate interest in the weal and woe of other creatures; their joys and sorrows, even their existence, are indifferent to him so long as he is not required indirectly (that is, by the excitement of his other impulses) to take them into consideration. And this is in fact the peculiar character-istic of the egoist—*inconsiderateness*. It is not the fact that he follows his special impulses that makes him hateful and blamable, but that he does so quite untroubled by the desires and needs of others. When he pursues his ends with such incon-siderateness that he coldly ignores the joys and sorrows of his neighbors (in so far as he sees no connection with his own aims), when he remains deaf and blind and cold to the happiness and misfortune of his neighbor, then we consider him to be an egoist, and frequently so even when otherwise we do not in the least condemn his aims.

Thus, in principle, we discover the nature of that tendency which we call by the reproachful name of selfishness; it is constituted by inconsiderateness, which is based upon the fact that among the existing inclinations the altruistic ones are relatively underdeveloped. It would, obviously, be vain labor to try to determine separately and exactly the relationship of impulses that must hold in order to designate a man as egoistic, or to ascribe to him a definite degree of this quality. Here we cannot distinguish strictly or discriminate exactly, not to speak of measuring, for we have to do throughout with vague concepts. In ethical statements we never get beyond relative, vague, qualitative comparisons. It is necessary to keep this in mind so that we may not hunt for an apparent exactness at the wrong place, which can lead to nothing but delusion. . . .

C. D. Broad

EGOISM AS A THEORY OF HUMAN MOTIVES

Reprinted from pp. 218–31 of *Ethics and the History of Philosophy*, by C. D. Broad (1952), by permission of the publishers, Routledge and Kegan Paul, Ltd. Charlie Dunbar Broad (1887–1971) was for many years a fellow of Trinity College, Cambridge University. He wrote on many philosophical problems, ranging over a wide spectrum of areas of philosophy, including ethics, the history of philosophy, epistemology, and the philosophy of science. Among his more important works are: *Five Types of Ethical Theory; The Mind and Its Place in Nature; Perception, Physics, and Reality;* and *Scientific Thought.*

There seem *prima facie* to be a number of different kinds of ultimate desire which all or most men have. Plausible examples would be the desire to get pleasant experiences and to avoid unpleasant ones, the desire to get and exercise power over others, and the desire to do what is right and to avoid doing what is wrong. Very naturally philosophers have tried to reduce this plurality. They have tried to show that there is one and only one kind of ultimate desire, and that all other desires which seem at first sight to be ultimate are really subordinate to this. I shall call the view that there really

are several different kinds of ultimate desire *Pluralism of Ul-*
timate Desires, and I shall call the view that there is really
only one kind of ultimate desire *Monism of Ultimate Desires*.
Even if a person were a pluralist about ultimate desires, he
might hold that there are certain important features common to
all the different kinds of ultimate desire.
   Now much the most important theory on this subject is that
all kinds of ultimate desire are *egoistic*. This is not in itself necessarily a monistic theory. For there might be several
irreducibly different kinds of ultimate desire, even if they
were all egoistic. Moreover, there might be several irreducibly different, though not necessarily unrelated, senses of the
word 'egoistic'; and some desires might be egoistic in one
sense and some in another, even if all were egoistic in some
sense. But the theory often takes the special form that the
only kind of ultimate desire is the desire to get or to prolong
pleasant experiences, and to avoid or to cut short unpleasant
experiences, for oneself. That *is* a monistic theory. I shall
call the wider theory *Psychological Egoism*, and this special
form of it *Pscyhological Hedonism*. Psychological Egoism might
be true, even though psychological hedonism were false; but, if
psychological egoism be false, psychological hedonism cannot be
true.
   I shall now discuss Psychological Egoism. I think it best
to begin by enumerating all the kinds of desire that I can
think of which might reasonably be called 'egoistic' in one
sense or another.
   (1) Everyone has a special desire for the continued existence of himself in his present bodily life, and a special
dread of his own death. This may be called *Desire for Self-*
preservation. (2) Everyone desires to get and to prolong experiences of certain kinds, and to avoid and to cut short
experiences of certain other kinds, because the former are
pleasant to him and the latter unpleasant. This may be called
Desire for one's own Happiness. (3) Everyone desires to acquire, keep, and develop certain mental and bodily powers and
dispositions, and to avoid, get rid of, or check certain others.
In general he wants to be or to become a person of a certain
kind, and wants not to be or to become a person of certain
other kinds. This may be called *Desire to be a Self of a cer-*
tain kind. (4) Everyone desires to feel certain kinds of emotion towards himself and his own powers and dispositions, and
not to feel certain other kinds of reflexive emotion. This may
be called *Desire for Self-respect*. (5) Everyone desires to get
and to keep for himself the exclusive possession of certain material objects or the means of buying and keeping such objects.
This may be called *Desire to get and to keep Property*. (6)
Everyone desires to get and to exercise power over certain
other persons, so as to make them do what he wishes, regardless

of whether they wish it or not. This may be called *Desire for Self-assertion*. (7) Everyone desires that other persons shall believe certain things about him and feel certain kinds of emotion towards him. He wants to be noticed, to be respected by some, to be loved by some, to be feared by some, and so on. Under this head come the *Desire for Self-display*, for *Affection*, and so on.

Lastly, it must be noted that some desires, which are concerned primarily with other things or persons, either would not exist at all or would be very much weaker or would take a diferent form if it were not for the fact that those things or persons already stand in certain relations to oneself. I shall call such relations *egoistic motive-stimulants*. The following are among the most important of these. (i) The relation of ownership. If a person owns a house or a wife, e.g. he feels a much stronger desire to improve the house or to make the woman happy than if the house belongs to another or the woman is married to someone else. (ii) Blood-relationship. A person desires, e.g. the well-being of his own children much more strongly than that of other children. (iii) Relations of love and friendship. A person desires strongly, e.g. to be loved and respected by those whom he loves. He may desire only to be feared by those whom he hates. And he may desire only very mildly, if at all, to be loved and respected by those to whom he feels indifferent. (iv) The relationship of being fellow-members of an institution to which one feels loyalty and affection. Thus, e.g. an Englishman will be inclined to do services to another Englishman which he would not do for a foreigner, and an Old Etonian will be inclined to do services to another Old Etonian which he would not do for an Old Harrovian.

I think that I have now given a reasonably adequate list of motives and motive-stimulants which could fairly be called 'egoistic' in some sense or other. Our next business is to try to classify them and to consider their inter-relations.

(1) Let us begin by asking ourselves the following question. Which of these motives could act on a person if he had been the only person or thing that had ever existed? The answer is that he could still have had desires for *self-preservation*, for *his own happiness*, to be a *self of a certain kind*, and for *self-respect*. But he could not, unless he were under the delusion that there were other persons or things, have desires for *property*, for *self-assertion*, or for *self-display*. Nor could he have any of those desires which are stimulated by family or other alio-relative relationships. I shall call those desires, and only those, which could be felt by a person who knew or believed himself to be the only existent in the universe, *Self-confined*.

(2) Any desire which is not self-confined may be described as *extra-verted*; for the person who has such a desire is neces-

sarily considering, not only himself and his own qualities, dispositions, and states, but also some other thing or person. If the desire is egoistic, it will also be *intro-verted*; for the person who has such a desire will also be considering himself and his relations to that other person or thing, and this will be an essential factor conditioning his experience. Thus a self-confined desire is purely intro-verted, whilst a desire which is egoistic but not self-confined is both intro-verted and extra-verted. Now we may subdivide desires of the latter kind into two classes, according as the primary emphasis is on the former or the latter aspect. Suppose that the person is concerned primarily with himself and his own acts and experiences, and that he is concerned with the other thing or person only or mainly as an object of these acts or experiences or as the other term in a relationship to himself. Then I shall call the desire *Self-centred*. I shall use the term *Self-regarding* to include both desires which are self-centred and those which are self-confined. Under the head of self-centred desires come the desire for *property*, for *self-assertion*, for *self-display*, and for *affection*.

(3) Lastly, we come to desires which are both intro-verted and extra-verted, but where the primary emphasis is on the other person or thing and its states. Here the relationship of the other person or thing to oneself acts as a strong egoistic motive-stimulant, but one's primary desire is that the other person or thing shall be in a certain state. I will call such desires *Other-regarding*. A desire which is other-regarding, but involves an egoistic motive-stimulant, may be described as *Self-referential*. The desire of a mother to render services to her own children which she would not be willing to render to other children is an instance of a desire which is other-regarding but self-referential. So, too, is the desire of a man to inflict suffering on one who has injured him or one whom he envies.

Having thus classified the various kinds of egoistic desire, I will now say something about their inter-relations.

(1) It is obvious that self-preservation may be desired as a necessary condition of one's own happiness; since one cannot acquire or prolong pleasant experiences unless one continues to exist. So the desire for self-preservation *may* be subordinate to the desire for one's own happiness. But it seems pretty clear that a person often desires to go on living even when there is no prospect that the remainder of his life will contain a balance of pleasant over unpleasant experiences. This attitude is expressed very strongly in the loathsome lines of Maecenas which Seneca has handed down to posterity:

Debilem facito manu, debilem pede coxo
tuber adstrue gibberum, lubricos quate dentes;
vita dum superest, bene est; hanc mihi, vel acuta
si sedeam cruce, sustine.

(2) It is also obvious that property and power over others
may be desired as a means to self-preservation or to happiness.
So the desire to get and keep property, and the desire to get
and exert power over others, *may* be subordinate to the desire
for self-preservation or for one's own happiness. But it seems
fairly certain that the former desires are sometimes independent of the latter. Even if a person begins by desiring property or power only as a means—and it is very doubtful whether
we always do begin in that way—it seems plain that he often
comes to desire them for themselves, and to sacrifice happiness,
security, and even life for them. Any miser, and almost any
keen politician, provides an instance of this.

It is no answer to this to say that a person who desires
power or property enjoys the experiences of getting and exercising power or of amassing and owning property, and then to
argue that therefore his ultimate desire is to give himself
those pleasant experiences. The premise here is true, but the
argument is self-stultifying. The experiences in question are
pleasant to a person only in so far as he desires power or
property. This kind of pleasant experience presupposes desires
for something other than pleasant experiences, and therefore
the latter desires cannot be derived from desire for that kind
of pleasant experience.

Similar remarks apply to the desire for self-respect and
the desire for self-display. If one already desires to feel
certain emotions towards oneself, or to be the object of certain emotions in others, the experience of feeling those emotions or of knowing that others feel them towards one will be
pleasant, because it will be the fulfilment of a pre-existing
desire. But this kind of pleasure presupposes the existence of
these desires, and therefore they cannot be derived from the
desire for that kind of pleasure.

(3) Although the various kinds of egoistic desire cannot
be reduced to a single ultimate egoistic desire, e.g. the desire for one's own happiness, they are often very much mixed up
with each other. Take, e.g. the special desire which a mother
feels for the health, happiness, and prosperity of her children.
This is predominantly other-regarding, though it is self-
referential. The mother is directly attracted by the thought
of her child as surviving, as having good dispositions and
pleasant experiences, and as being the object of love and respect to other persons. She is directly repelled by the
thought of his dying, or having bad dispositions or unpleasant
experiences, or being the object of hatred or contempt to other

persons. The desire is therefore other-regarding. It is self-referential, because the fact that it is *her* child and not another's acts as a powerful motive-stimulant. She would not be prepared to make the same sacrifices for the survival or the welfare of a child which was not her own. But this self-referential other-regarding motive is almost always mingled with other motives which are self-regarding. One motive which a woman has for wanting her child to be happy, healthy and popular is the desire that other women shall envy her as the mother of a happy, healthy and popular child. This motive is subordinate to the self-centred desire for self-display. Another motive, which may be present, is the desire not to be burdened with an ailing, unhappy, and unpopular child. This motive is subordinate to the self-contained desire for one's own happiness. But, although the self-referential other-regarding motive is nearly always mixed with motives which are self-centred or self-confined, we cannot plausibly explain the behaviour of many mothers on many occasions towards their children without postulating the other-regarding motive.

We can now consider the various forms which Psychological Egoism might take. The most rigid form is that all human motives are ultimately egoistic, and that all egoistic motives are ultimately of one kind. That one kind has generally been supposed to be the desire for one's own happiness, and so this form of Psychological Egoism may in practice be identified with Psychological Hedonism. This theory amounts to saying that the only ultimate motives are *self-confined*, and that the only ultimate self-confined motive is *desire for one's own happiness*.

I have already tried to show by examples that this is false. Among self-confined motives, e.g. is the desire for self-preservation, and this cannot be reduced to desire for one's own happiness. Then, again, there are self-regarding motives which are self-centred but not self-confined, such as the desire for affection, for gratitude, for power over others, and so on. And, finally, there are motives which are self-referential but predominantly other-regarding, such as a mother's desire for her children's welfare or a man's desire to injure one whom he hates.

It follows that the only form of Psychological Egoism that is worth discussing is the following. It might be alleged that all ultimate motives are *either* self-confined *or* self-centred *or* other-regarding but self-referential, some being of one kind and some of another. This is a much more modest theory than, e.g. Psychological Hedonism. I think that it covers satisfactorily an immensely wide field of human motivation, but I am not sure that it is true without exception. I shall now discuss it in the light of some examples.

Case A. Take first the case of a man who does not expect to survive the death of his present body, and who makes a will,

the contents of which will be known to no one during his life-
time.

(1) The motive of such a testator cannot possibly be the
expectation of any experiences which he will enjoy after death
through the provisions of his will being carried out; for he
believes that he will have no more experiences after the death
of his body. The only way in which this motive could be
ascribed to such a man is by supposing that, although he is
intellectually convinced of his future extinction, yet in
practice he cannot help imagining himself as surviving and wit-
nessing events which will happen after his death. I think that
this kind of mental confusion is possible, and perhaps not un-
common; but I should doubt whether it is a plausible account of
such a man's motives to say that they all involve this mistake.

(2) Can we say that his motive is the desire to enjoy
during his life the pleasant experience of imagining the gratitude which the beneficiaries will feel towards him after his
death? The answer is that this may well be *one* of his motives,
but it cannot be primary, and therefore cannot be the only one.
Unless he desired to be thought about in one way rather than
another after his death, the present experience of imagining
himself as becoming the object of certain retrospective
thoughts and emotions on the part of the beneficiaries would be
neither attractive nor repulsive to him.

(3) I think it is plain, then, that the ultimate motive of
such a man cannot be desire for his own happiness. But it
might be desire for power over others. For he may be said to
be exercising this power when he makes his will, even though
the effects will not begin until after his death.

(4) Can we say that his motive in making the will is simply to ensure that certain persons will think about him and
feel towards him in certain ways after his death? In that case
his motive would come under the head of self-display. (This
must, of course, be distinguished from the question, already
discussed, whether his motive might be to give himself the pleasant experience of imagining their future feelings of gratitude
towards him.) The answer is that self-display, in a wide sense,
may be a motive, and a very strong one, in making a will; but
it could hardly be the sole motive. A testator generally considers the relative needs of various possible beneficiaries,
the question whether a certain person would appreciate and take
care of a certain picture or house or book, the question
whether a certain institution is doing work which he thinks important, and so on. In so far as he is influenced by these
considerations, his motives are other-regarding. But they may
all be self-referential. In making his will he may desire to
benefit persons only in so far as they are *his* relatives or
friends. He may desire to benefit institutions only in so far
as *he* is or has been a member of them. And so on. I think

that it would be quite plausible to hold that the motives of such a testator are all either self-regarding or self-referential, but that it would not be in the least plausible to say that they are all self-confined or that none of them are other-regarding.

Case B. Let us next consider the case of a man who subscribes anonymously to a certain charity. His motive cannot possibly be that of self-display. Can we say that his motive is to enjoy the pleasant experience of self-approval and of seeing an institution in which he is interested flourishing? The answer is, again, that these motives may exist and may be strong, but they cannot be primary and therefore cannot be his only motives. Unless he wants the institution to flourish, there will be nothing to attract him in the experience of seeing it flourish. And, unless he subscribes from some other motive than the desire to enjoy a feeling of self-approval, he will not obtain a feeling of self-approval. So here, again, it seems to me that some of his motives must be other-regarding. But it is quite possible that his other-regarding motives may all be self-referential. An essential factor in making him want to benefit this institution may be that it is *his* old college or that a great friend of *his* is at the head of it.

The question, then, that remains is this. Are there any cases in which it is reasonable to think that a person's motive is not egoistic in any of the senses mentioned? In practice, as we now see, this comes down to the question whether there are any cases in which an other-regarding motive is not stimulated by an egoistic motive-stimulus, i.e. whether there is any other-regarding motive which is not also and essentially self-referential.

Case C. Let us consider the case of a person who deliberately chooses to devote his life to working among lepers, in the full knowledge that he will almost certainly contract leprosy and die in a particularly loathsome way. This is not an imaginary case. To give the Psychological Egoist the longest possible run for his money I will suppose that the person is a Roman Catholic priest, who believes that his action may secure for him a place in heaven in the next world and a reputation for sanctity and heroism in this, that it may be rewarded posthumously with canonization, and that it will redound to the credit of the church of which he is an ordained member.

It is difficult to see what self-regarding or self-referential motives there could be *for* the action beside desire for happiness in heaven, desire to gain a reputation for sanctity and heroism and perhaps to be canonized after death, and desire to glorify the church of which one is a priest. Obviously there are extremely strong self-confined and self-centred motives *against* choosing this kind of life. And in many cases there must have been very strong self-referential other-regard-

ing motives *against* it. For the person who made such a choice
must sometimes have been a young man of good family and bril-
liant prospects, whose parents were heart-broken at his decision, and whose friends thought him an obstinate fool for
making it.

Now there is no doubt at all that there was an other-
regarding motive, viz. a direct desire to alleviate the sufferings of the lepers. No one who was not dying in the last ditch
for an over-simple theory of human nature would deny this. The
only questions that are worth raising about it are these. (1)
Is this other-regarding motive stimulated by an egoistic motive-
stimulus and thus rendered self-referential? (2) Suppose that
this motive had not been supported by the various self-regarding and self-referential motives *for* deciding to go and work
among the lepers, would it have sufficed, in presence of the
motives *against* doing so, to ensure the choice that was actually made?

As regards the first question, I cannot see that there was
any special pre-existing relationship between a young priest in
Europe and a number of unknown lepers in Asia which might plausibly be held to act as an egoistic motive-stimulus. The lepers
are neither his relatives nor his friends nor his benefactors
nor members of any community or institution to which he belongs.

As regards the sufficiency of the other-regarding motive,
whether stimulated egoistically or not, in the absence of all
self-regarding motives tending in the same direction, no conclusive answer can be given. I cannot prove that a single person in the whole course of history *would* have decided to work
among lepers, if all the motives against doing so had been present, whilst the hope of heaven, the desire to gain a reputation
for sanctity and heroism, and the desire to glorify and extend
one's church had been wholly absent. Nor can the Psychological
Egoist prove that *no* single person would have so decided under
these hypothetical conditions. Factors which cannot be elimi-
nated cannot be shown to be necessary and cannot be shown to be
superfluous; and there we must leave the matter.

I suspect that a Psychological Egoist might be tempted to
say that the intending medical missionary found the experience
of imagining the sufferings of the lepers intensely unpleasant,
and that his primary motive for deciding to spend his life
working among them was to get rid of this unpleasant experience. This, I think, is what Locke, e.g. would have had to
say in accordance with his theory of motivation. About this
suggestion there are two remarks to be made.

(1) This motive cannot have been primary, and therefore
cannot have been the only motive. Unless this person desired
that the lepers should have their sufferings alleviated, there
is no reason why the thought of their sufferings should be an
unpleasant experience to him. A malicious man, e.g. finds the

thought of the sufferings of an enemy a very pleasant experience. This kind of pleasure presupposes a desire for the well-being or the ill-being of others.

(2) If his primary motive were to rid himself of the unpleasant experience of imagining the sufferings of the lepers, he could hardly choose a less effective means than to go and work among them. For the imagination would then be replaced by actual sense-perception; whilst, if he stayed at home and devoted himself to other activities, he would have a reasonably good chance of diverting his attention from the sufferings of the lepers. In point of fact one knows that such a person would reproach himself in so far as he managed to forget about the lepers. He would *wish* to keep them and their sufferings constantly in mind, as an additional stimulus to doing what he believes he ought to do, viz. to take active steps to help and relieve them.

In this connexion it is important to notice the following facts. For most people the best way to realize the sufferings of strangers is to imagine oneself or one's parents or children or some intimate and beloved friend in the situation in which the stranger is placed. This, as we say, 'brings home to one' his sufferings. A large proportion of the cruelty which decent people applaud or tolerate is applauded or tolerated by them only because they are either too stupid to put themselves imaginatively into the position of the victims or because they deliberately refrain from doing so. One important cause of their deliberately refraining is the notion of retributive justice, i.e. the belief that these persons, or a group taken as a collective whole to which they belong, have *deserved* suffering by wrongdoing, and the desire that they shall get their deserts. Another important cause of this deliberate refrainment is the knowledge that one is utterly powerless to help the victims. However this may be, the fact that imagining oneself in their position is often a necessary condition of desiring to relieve the sufferings of strangers does not make that desire self-referential. Imagining oneself in their place is merely a condition for becoming vividly *aware of* their sufferings. Whether one will then desire to relieve them or to prolong them or will remain indifferent to them, depends on motives which are not primarily self-regarding or self-referential.

I will now summarize the results of this discussion.

(1) If Psychological Egoism asserts that all ultimate motives are self-confined; or that they are all either self-confined or self-centred, some being of one kind and some of the other; or that all self-confined motives can be reduced to the desire for one's own happiness; it is certainly false. It is not even a close approximation to the truth.

(2) If it asserts that all ultimate motives are either self-regarding or self-referential, some being of one kind and

some of the other; and that all other-regarding motives require a self-referential stimulus, it is a close approximation to the truth. It is true, I think, that in most people and at most times other-regarding motives are very weak unless stimulated by a self-referential stimulus. As England's wisest and wittiest statesman put it in his inimitable way: 'Temporal things will have their weight in the world, and, though zeal may prevail for a time and get the better in a skirmish, yet the war endeth generally on the side of flesh and blood, and will do so until mankind is another thing than it is at present.'[1]

(3) Nevertheless, Psychological Egoism, even in its most diluted form, is very doubtful if taken as a universal proposition. Some persons at some times are strongly influenced by other-regarding motives which cannot plausibly be held to be stimulated by a self-referential stimulus. It seems reasonable to hold that the presence of these other-regarding motives is *necessary* to account for their choice of alternatives which they do choose, and for their persistence in the course which they have adopted, though this can never be conclusively established in any particular case. Whether it is also *sufficient* cannot be decided with certainty, for self-regarding and self-referential components are always present in one's total motive for choosing such an action.

I think that the summary which I have just given fairly represents the results of introspection and reflection on one's own and other men's voluntary action. Yet Psychological Egoism in general and Psychological Hedonism in particular have seemed almost self-evident to many highly intelligent thinkers, and they do still seem highly plausible to nearly everyone when he first begins to speculate on human motivation. I believe that this depends, not on empirical facts, but on certain verbal ambiguities and misunderstandings. As so often happens in philosophy, clever people accept a false general principle on *a priori* grounds and then devote endless labour and ingenuity to explaining away plain facts which obviously conflict with it. A full discussion of the subject would require an analysis of the confusions which have made these theories seem so plausible; but this must be omitted here.

I must content myself with the following remarks in conclusion. I have tried to show that Psychological Egoism, in the only form in which it could possibly fit the facts of human life, is not a monistic theory of motives. On this extended interpretation of the theory the only feature common to all motives is that every motive which can *act on* a person has one or another of a large number of different kinds of special *reference to* that person. I have tried to show that this certainly

---

[1]Halifax: *The Character of a Trimmer.*

covers a very wide field, but that it is by no means certain that there is even this amount of unity among *all* human motives. I think that Psychological Egoism is much the most plausible attempt to reduce the *prima facie* plurality of ultimate kinds of desire to a unity. If it fails, I think it is most unlikely that any alternative attempt on a different basis will succeed.

For my part I am inclined to accept an irreducibly pluralistic view of human motives. This does not, of course, entail that the present irreducible plurality of ultimate motives may not have evolved, in some sense of that highly ambiguous word, out of fewer, either in the history of each individual or in that of the human race. About that I express no opinion here and now.

Now, if Psychological Hedonism had been true, all conflict of motives would have been between motives of the *same kind*. It would always be of the form 'Shall I go to the dentist and certainly be hurt now but probably avoid thereby frequent and prolonged toothache in future? Or shall I take the risk in order to avoid the certainty of being hurt by the dentist now?' On any pluralistic view there is also conflict between motives of irreducibly *different kinds*, e.g. between aversion to painful experience and desire to be thought manly, or between a desire to shine in conversation and aversion to hurting a sensitive person's feelings by a witty but wounding remark.

It seems to me plain that, in our ordinary moral judgments about ourselves and about others, we always unhesitatingly assume that there can be and often is conflict between motives of radically different kinds. Now I do not myself share that superstitious reverence for the beliefs of common sense which many contemporary philosophers profess. But I think that we must start from them, and that we ought to depart from them only when we find good reason to do so. If Psychological Hedonism, or any other monistic theory of motives had been true, we should have had to begin the study of Ethics by recognizing that most moral judgments which we pass on ourselves or on others are made under a profound misapprehension of the psychological facts and are largely vitiated thereby. If Psychological Hedonism, e.g. had been true, the only ethical theory worth discussing would have been an egoistic form of Ethical Hedonism. For one cannot be under an obligation to attempt to do what is psychologically impossible. And, on the hypothesis of Psychological Hedonism, it is psychologically impossible for anyone ultimately to desire anything except to prolong or acquire experiences which he knows or expects to be pleasant and to cut short or avoid experiences which he knows or expects to be unpleasant. If it were still possible to talk of having duties at all, each person's duties would be confined within the limits which that psychological impossibility marks out. And it

would clearly be impossible to suppose that any part of anyone's ultimate motive for doing any act is his belief that it
would be right in the circumstances together with his desire to
do what is right as such. For, if Psychological Hedonism were
true, a desire to do what is right could not be ultimate, it
must be subordinate to the desire to get or prolong pleasant experiences and to avoid or cut short unpleasant ones.

Now it is plain that such consequences as these conflict
sharply with common-sense notions of morality. If we had been
obliged to accept Psychological Egoism, in any of its narrower
forms, on its merits, we should have had to say: 'So much the
worse for the common-sense notions of morality!' But, if I am
right, the morality of common sense, with all its difficulties
and incoherences, is immune at least to attacks from the basis
of Psychological Egoism.

Michael A. Slote

AN EMPIRICAL BASIS FOR PSYCHOLOGICAL EGOISM

This is a revised version of "An Empirical Basis for
Psychological Egoism," which was published in *The
Journal of Philosophy* 61, no. 18 (October 1, 1964).
It is reprinted here by permission of *The Journal of
Philosophy* and the author. Michael A. Slote is a
member of the department of philosophy, State Uni-
versity of New York at Stony Brook. He is the author
of *Reason and Scepticism*, published in 1970.

It is commonly believed in the philosophical world today
that the age-old problem of psychological egoism is merely a
pseudo-problem and that this is true just because the a priori
philosophical arguments that have traditionally been given in
favor of egoism depend in the main upon confusions about the
logic of our ordinary language. It has been claimed, for example, that the well-known argument that we act selfishly even
when we want to help others because in such cases we are still
attempting to *satisfy our own desire* to help others, is falla-
ciously generated by misunderstandings of the proper use of
terms like 'want', 'satisfy', and 'desire'.[1]

---

[1]See P. H. Nowell-Smith's *Ethics* (New York: Philosophical Li-
brary, 1957), ch. 10, *passim*.

In *Butler's Moral Philosophy*, Austin Duncan-Jones, expressing Butler's view, and, it seems from the context, his own as well, states that if there is something wrong with all the a priori philosophical arguments that have traditionally been given in favor of egoism (which he has earlier identified with the doctrine that all human acts are selfish),[2] then there is little else to recommend the theory, since "the appearance of things, undistorted by theory," is that men sometimes do act unselfishly, disinterestedly. Only one who already believed in the validity of the philosophical arguments for egoism would have any reason to interpret the facts of human behavior in a way compatible with the doctrine of egoism.[3] Thus Duncan-Jones seems clearly to be ruling out the possibility that the (empirical) facts as they stand could, with any semblance of objectivity, be used to support egoism. And many other contemporary philosophers would, I think, tend to agree with him.

In the present paper I wish to argue that psychological egoism may well have a basis in the empirical facts of human psychology. Certain contemporary learning theorists, e.g., Hull and Skinner, have put forward behavioristic theories of the origin and functioning of human motives which posit a certain number of basically "selfish," unlearned primary drives or motives (like hunger, thirst, sleep, elimination, and sex), explain all other, higher-order, drives or motives as derived genetically from the primary ones via certain "laws of reinforcement," and, further, deny the "functional autonomy" of those higher-order drives or motives.[4] Now it is a hotly debated issue in contemporary Learning Theory whether any theory such as we have described briefly above could adequately explain adult human behavior. I shall, however, argue only that a theory of the above kind may well be true, and that from such

---

[2]It has been suggested to me by P. R. Foot that only those of one's acts which are somehow related to the wants or interests of others can correctly be called either selfish or unselfish. If this be so, then Duncan-Jones' definition of egoism will make that doctrine trivially false, just because there are some human actions that are neither selfish nor unselfish. In order to avoid such an eventuality, *I* shall mean by *egoism* the slightly different thesis (perhaps more accurately, but clumsily, designated *non-altruism*) that no human act is ever *unselfish*.

[3]See p. 109 of *Butler's Moral Philosophy*.

[4]It will not, I think, be necessary for my purposes to be truer to ordinary language or more precise with the concepts of drive and motive than are the learning theorists themselves. Thus, e.g., I shall be using 'drive' and 'motive' interchangeably in this paper.

a theory, fortified only by one additional psychological premise, the truth of egoism (non-altruism) logically follows. I
hope to show, thereby, that the question of psychological egoism is still an open empirical issue, however fallacious be the
philosophical arguments for it.

But what is "functional autonomy," and how does the lack
of it help to show our actions to be selfish? According to behavioristic learning psychologists a higher-order (acquired)
motive is functionally autonomous when it becomes causally independent of primary motives (especially of those motives association with which enabled it to be acquired in the first
place) in such a way that one will indefinitely keep acting
from that motive, even if rewards for those other, primary, motives are no longer in general associated with such action.[5]
We have reason to believe that a higher-order drive or motive
is *not* functionally autonomous, i.e., is functionally dependent,
if when we cut off all reinforcement of it by primary rewards
(rewards of primary drives) and there are, in addition, both a
sufficient number of "extinction trials" (occurrences of acts
done from that higher-order motive which are not associated
even indirectly, i.e., through other higher-order motives, with
primary rewards) and a complete absence, during those extinction trials, of primary rewards for any similar higher-order
motives (to eliminate the possibility of generalization of primary rewards from motives other than that being extinguished),
the higher-order drive or motive actually does extinguish; i.e.,
the person whose higher-order motive is being extinguished
eventually, even if perhaps only very gradually, ceases to act
from that higher-order motive.

It is necessary for a motive *derived genetically* from
"selfish" (or at least not *unselfish*) primary drives also to be
functionally dependent upon them if we are to be able to say
that acts performed from that motive are never unselfish. For
the fact that in the past we performed such acts only because
they led to the satisfaction of some other non-unselfish motive
or motives, i.e., because they were reinforced by primary-drive
rewards, does not show that such acts performed *now* are not unselfish. To argue thus would be indeed to commit a "genetic
fallacy." An act must *presently* be causally connected with
drives that are not unselfish in order to be considered selfish.
Now those who deny functional autonomy are saying in effect
that whenever, e.g., one acts benevolently (i.e., from what the

---

[5]I have given a very brief account of the notions of primary
and higher-order drives or motives; but it should be sufficient
for the purposes of this paper. A more complete account of
these and of the other psychological notions I make use of can
be found in practically any textbook of experimental psychology.

psychologist would call the higher-order motive of benevolence), one is performing that act, or at least, in general performing acts of that kind, only because such benevolent action is in general still associated with and reinforced by the satisfaction of such non-unselfish primary drives as hunger and thirst, whether those drives be the same as or different from the primary drives from which the motive of benevolence actually originated.

I do not, however, wish to maintain that the hypothesis of functional dependence (together with its learning-theoretical underpinnings) entails egoism all by itself. The hypothesis does, indeed, entail that we continue to act "benevolently" or "self-sacrificingly" only because such action on our part is in general reinforced by the rewarding of selfish primary drives. But is it not possible that the primary rewards received, in general, when one acts benevolently or self-sacrificingly are not so great as those relinquished in the doing of such acts? It might, in other words, be the case that a poverty-stricken mother who sacrificed some of her own food so that her child might eat better acted in this way only because she was, in general, receiving (however indirectly) some primary-drive satisfactions for her sacrifices. And yet we would still call her actions unselfish if we thought that the rewards she was sacrificing (reduction of her hunger) were greater than those she was getting in return; for is not the habit of giving more than one asks in return an exemplary case of unselfishness?

I should like now to show that a certain empirical hypothesis that entails the hypothesis of functional dependence also entails the thesis of psychological egoism and rules out the possibility of a case like the above, even if the hypothesis of functional dependence taken alone does not.[6]

Let us imagine that we have a method for determining empirically which primary rewards a person prefers to which others. We set up various situations where the man has to choose between primary rewards, situations involving no moral factors and no interests of other people, and determine the man's preferences. A learning theorist might claim that it is true as a matter of empirical fact that whenever a man systematically (i.e., as a general rule) continues to sacrifice primary reward x to other people, he does so only because he usually obtains thereby some primary reward y *and* because y ranks higher than x on the person's preference scorecard, as deter-

---

[6]I am again indebted to Mrs. Foot for the insight that the hypothesis of functional dependence does not itself, alone, entail that no act is unselfish. In addition, I am indebted to discussion with Prof. R. P. Wolff for some of the points I shall be making hereafter—and to Prof. T. Nagel for some important clarifications.

mined in situations where no considerations of other people's
interests and thus of sacrifice to other people's interests
were involved.[7] And the above empirical claim, which involves,
but is not exhausted by, the claim that functional dependence
is true, entails, I think, the thesis of psychological egoism.
For if our conscious acts of benevolence and sympathy and sacrifice, etc., are continuing to be performed by us only because
we do not, in performing those acts, in general give away *less*
in the way of primary-drive satisfactions than we actually get
in return, the inevitable conclusion would be that all our acts
were fundamentally (or ultimately or "really") motivated by our
"selfish" primary drives. If this were the case, then, indeed,
none of our actions would ever "really" or fundamentally or
ultimately be unselfish. The above-described case of the
mother who gives away more in the way of primary-drive satisfaction than she gets for herself in return would just never
come up. Psychological egoism would be true.

We have thus shown that egoism (in our sense) would be
true if certain psychological hypotheses turned out to be true
and that the question of the truth of psychological egoism is
an empirical question. But that is not to say that contemporary psychology has been able to prove the truth of these hypotheses or that psychologists are even all agreed that, with
the further advancement of psychology as a science, these hypotheses will as a matter of fact be verified. There are many
pyschologists who think, for example, that some higher-order
drives *do* become functionally autonomous. Gordon Allport, for
instance, has brought to light a good deal of psychological
evidence in favor of this contention.[8] Furthermore, the hypothesis of functional dependence is very difficult to establish
experimentally, for reasons well known to psychologists. In
the words of Neal Miller, "a strong learned drive may seem unaffected for many [extinction] trials and still eventually extinguish. When generalization, higher-order reinforcement, and
shifts from one reinforcing agent to another are added to this
possibility, it can be seen how difficult it is in complex human situations to determine whether a habit [drive] actually is
functionally autonomous."[9] In other words, even if there is no

---

[7]Of course, there are some primary rewards, like sexual gratification, that are very hard to measure in isolation from all
moral considerations.

[8]See his *Personality: a Psychological Interpretation.*

[9]"Learnable Drives and Rewards," in S. S. Stevens, ed., *Hand-
book of Experimental Psychology*, p. 469.
        See also D. C. McClelland, "Functional Autonomy of Motives
as an Extinction Phenomenon," *Psychological Review*, 49 (1942):
272-283.

functional autonomy, there are many ways in which a functionally dependent drive might *appear* to be autonomous, because of
distorting psychological factors that can never with absolute
certainty be ruled out in the context of human motivation.
However, the question whether some drive is autonomous is still
empirical in principle, however difficult it may be in practice,
given the current rudimentary state of the science of psychology, to determine whether that drive would extinguish if its association with primary reinforcements were entirely severed.

Consider also the hypothesis that entails both functional
dependence and egoism, the hypothesis, namely, that even if
people sometimes do sacrifice and continue to sacrifice a certain kind of primary reward, they only do so because they in
general get some greater primary reward in return. This hypothesis, I think, might also turn out to be empirically false. It
might turn out, for example, that, although people never made
sacrifices unless they got something in return, they sometimes
sacrificed some primary reward x for some other primary reward
y even though y ranked lower on their preference scorecard as
determined in morally neutral circumstances. In such a case
there are two things we can say. We might well say that the
scorecard as determined in morally neutral circumstances does
not tell us a man's real preferences, for if he prefers x to y
in neutral circumstances, but prefers y to x when certain other
people's interests are involved, who can say what his real
preference is? We might, on the other hand, want to say that
what a man prefers in morally neutral circumstances really does
tell us fairly accurately what he *really* prefers, so that if
his preferences differ where moral considerations are involved,
we have a right to say that the man has, in the interests of
morality, gone against his own preferences and made an unselfish sacrifice. Whether we should want to say the first or
the second of these things would depend a great deal, I think,
on a number of other scientifically relevant factors. Anyone
who would *in principle* refuse to say the second kind of thing
would in effect be considering it to be tautologously true that
men do not persist in acting against their own self-interest;
that is, he would be making the thesis of egoism into a mere
tautology, which, I prefer to think, it is not. It seems that
there very well could be circumstances in which it would from
a scientific point of view be advisable to say that a man had
acted against his own real preferences, had persistently sacrificed a greater for a smaller primary reward out of a sense of
duty or a feeling of benevolence. Such circumstances might
exist, for example, if we had a detailed knowledge of brain
physiology which showed that the brain contained a "preference"
center and a "morality" center and that the morality center affected our actions not by directly influencing the preference
center, but, rather, by acting as an inhibitor or as a modifier

on certain motor impulses sent out by the preference center.
Such a physiological theory would make it eminently plausible,
I think, to believe that what we did in moral contexts might
consistently go against our real preferences. In terms of such
a theory, then, it might be possible empirically to refute the
hypothesis that we never consistently or systematically sacrifice the greater for the smaller primary reward. Thus it would
seem that both "parts" of that psychological theory which, I
have claimed, entails psychological egoism, are open to empirical refutation, as well as confirmation.[10]

The psychological theory I have been describing should not
be confused with a certain theory of human behavior and motivation put forward in recent years by the psychologist A. H. Maslow, a theory which, I believe, does *not* entail psychological
egoism. According to Maslow people will not act from such
higher motives as benevolence and love unless certain lower
needs like hunger, safety, and elimination have already to some
degree been satisfied. But once physiological and other lower
needs are satisfied to a reasonable degree, needs to be benevolent, creative, loving, self-sacrificial, and the like will
spring up of their own accord. And one will continue to act
benevolently, creatively, etc., just as long as one's lower
needs remain satisfied, even if none of one's benevolent or
creative activities is actually reinforced by the satisfaction
of lower needs (primary drives).[11]

Clearly this theory differs substantially from the one I
have been describing. For it does *not* assert that we will persist in acting benevolently, etc., only if such acts are in general associated with the satisfaction of selfish primary drives.
It says merely that we require a certain amount of primary-
drive contentment if we are to become people who constantly act
benevolently *whether we are rewarded for doing so or not*. According to Maslow, a man often will habitually act from benevolence even though there is "nothing in it for him." It is
clear, then, that his theory does *not* exclude the possibility
of unselfish human action. The theory *we* have been discussing,
on the other hand, does exclude that possibility, just because
it implies that we persist in performing some kind of action
only because there is in general something in it for us.

---

[10]There is indeed still another way we have not yet mentioned
in which this psychological theory might empirically be refuted,
namely, if some theory (like Hume's) which made benevolence or
other unselfish motives into basic human instincts (primary
drives) turned out to be correct.

[11]See Maslow's *Motivation and Personality*, ch. 5, *passim*.

It would seem, then, that, as psychology stands today, there is at least some reason to think that the psychological theory we have been discussing may be true. Consequently, the truth of psychological egoism is still an open empirical question. Duncan-Jones and others are mistaken in their belief that, now that the a priori arguments for egoism seem to have been shown to be fallacious, no further case can possibly be made in its favor. Perhaps the only reason philosophers are thus mistaken is their ignorance of contemporary Learning Theory, its issues, and its results.[12] It is interesting to note, furthermore, that it is impossible to object to an empirical argument for egoism, the way one so often objects to a priori arguments for egoism, by saying that such arguments end up depriving 'selfish' of the logical possibility of a contrast, thus rendering the word meaningless. For egoism will be false if either part of the psychological theory we have been discussing is false. Thus, in making the truth of egoism depend on the truth of an empirically falsifiable psychological theory, I am leaving open at the very least the *logical* possibility that egoism is false, that some acts are unselfish.

I might add, finally, that the explanation I have attempted to give of the possibility of arguing on an empirical basis for egoism may help us to understand why so many people, especially beginning students of philosophy, are so dissatisfied by attempts to discredit egoism by showing the invalidity of the traditional philosophical arguments that have been put forward to prove it, and why the doctrine of egoism keeps cropping up, however many be the philosophical voices that seek to silence it. I am willing to conjecture that egoism will not lie dead, because people in some way see that there may be more in favor of egoism than *a priori arguments*. It is my very tentative suggestion that the reason for this may be that even those with little or no training in psychology believe, however inarticulately, that something like the psychological theory we have been discussing in this paper may well be true, believe that men who act consistently in a benevolent manner, for example, are acting benevolently only because their selfish desires and/or interests are usually satisfied by their doing so.

---

[12]I do not, however, wish to suggest that *psychologists* have been totally unaware of the philosophical consequences of their own theories. See, for example, Allport, *op. cit.*, p. 206.

Justin Aronfreed

ALTRUISTIC BEHAVIOR

From *Conduct and Conscience* (New York and London: Academic Press, 1968), pp. 138-49. Reprinted with the
permission of Academic Press and the author. Readers
who desire a fuller appreciation of this selection
should consult chapters 3 and 4 of *Conduct and Conscience*, "The Concept of Internalization" and "Mechanisms of Socialization." References by Aronfreed to
other works have been left in this selection, but for
the works cited the interested reader should consult
the bibliography at the end of *Conduct and Conscience*
(which will also give the reader an extensive acquaintance with the literature of psychology relevant to the
topics of egoism and altruism). Justin Aronfreed is
professor of psychology and director of the doctoral
program in developmental psychology at the University
of Pennsylvania. He has conducted experiments and
written extensively on the psychology of moral behavior.

Altruistic and sympathetic behavior are identified more
accurately by the conditions under which they occur than they
are by the specific forms which they may assume. Although
the identifying criteria for these two types of conduct can
be made quite distinct, it sometimes happens that one act will
meet both sets of criteria. Both altruistic and sympathetic
behavior may be acquired through either behavior-contingent or
observational learning. And their mechanisms of acquisition
engage both positive and aversive affective control. But their
socialization is always dependent on the prerequisite establishment of the child's capacity for empathic and vicarious experience.

It is often assumed that altruistic acts are independent
of their reinforcing consequences for the actor (see, for example, Durkheim, 1951, pp. 217-240). If this assumption were tak-
en quite literally, the criterion that it would impose on altruistic behavior would be inconsistent with the more general theoretical constraints which we find necessary to an account of
socialization. From the point of view of a conception of socialization that is grounded on affective as well as cognitive
control of the child's behavior, we must assume that an altruistic act is responsive to the affective value of its antici-
pated outcomes, and that it often has reinforcing consequences

for the actor. The control of altruistic behavior cannot be an
exception to the mechanisms which appear to govern all other
kinds of social conduct. Nor is this assumption contradicted
even by the fact that an altruistic act may have directly aversive consequences for the actor, since the performance of the
act can always be taken to indicate that its total outcome
structure is preferred to the outcomes of an alternative act.
Irwin's (1961) analysis of the concept of preference could be
extended here in order to illustrate how the outcomes of an
altruistic act might be directly aversive to the actor, and yet
might be preferred to the outcomes of another act that was not
altruistic.

     The assertion that an altruistic act must be sustained by
its consequences for the actor does not commit us to the view
that altruism is simply another manifestation of the rules
which govern the mutual exchange and distribution of social re-
sources. Such a view has been espoused in some analyses of
social behavior. (Gouldner, 1960; Homans, 1961; Thibaut and
Kelley, 1959). But when we say that an act displays altruism,
we assert that the choice of the act, in preference to an alternative act, is at least partly determined by the actor's expectation of consequences which will benefit another person
rather than himself. This assertion does not imply that the
consequences for the other person will have no affective value
for the actor. Nor does it imply that an altruistic component
of behavior can be maintained without reinforcing consequences.
An act may have reinforcing consequences without having directly beneficial outcomes for the actor. The reinforcement of the
act may be mediated either by its concretely visible consequences for another person or by the actor's cognitive representation of such consequences. For example, as a result of
earlier social conditioning, people may come to experience altruistic pleasure in response to their own actions, through
their capacity to represent to themselves the effect which
their actions will have on another person (even when the effect
may not be directly observable). The affective value of such
cognitive representations may also be determined by the more
complex normative and self-evaluative systems which people can
apply to the consequences of their behavior for others.

     Regardless of whether the effects of an act on another
person are directly observed or are given a cognitive representation, they can function as reinforcing outcomes for the actor
to the extent that their affective value is transmitted through
the actor's empathic or vicarious experience. Empathic or vicarious control of behavior is in fact a requirement of the
truly altruistic act. The initial establishment of altruistic
dispositions in the young child takes place when the child's
empathic or vicarious experience permits certain forms of its
behavior to be reinforced by the visibly pleasurable or dis-

tress-reducing consequences which they have for others. As the cognitive capacities of the child expand in the course of development, the affective value that can be carried by representational cognition becomes an increasingly available source of potential support for its altruistic behavior. But even when the child can give extensive cognitive representation and evaluation to the consequences of its behavior, the altruistic component of the behavior is still dependent on the child's capacity for empathic or vicarious experience. Since the altruistic property of an act is defined in part by the absence of directly beneficial consequences for the actor, it may always be regarded as being under some degree of internalized control. Of course, an altruistic act may be said to have an even more highly internalized status when its empathic or vicarious reinforcement is mediated by a cognitive representation that does not require its consequences for others to be directly observable.

    There has been an interesting recent development in the use of the concept of altruism by ethologists who have argued that natural selection favors a certain amount of behavior that has beneficial consequences for another member of the same species (Hamilton, 1964; Wynne-Edwards, 1962). The general line of argument is that there may be some adaptive advantage in the evolution of unlearned behavioral dispositions which are altruistic in the sense that they benefit others, even at some disadvantage to the individual—for example, alarm calls at the approach of predators (Maynard Smith, 1965)—particularly if the doner and the recipient of the advantage have a close genetic relationship. Comparative psychologists also occasionally have speculated that there might be certain innate dispositions toward the acquisition of altruistic behavior, which are especially visible at the highest phylogenetic levels (Hebb and Thompson, 1954; McBride and Hebb, 1948)—as evidenced, for example, in reactions to the distress of others. Campbell (1965) has suggested that human beings also may have strong unlearned altruistic dispositions, particularly toward others whom they perceive as similar to themselves, and that these dispositions have been selected for their adaptive value in meeting environmental stresses. There also have been other advocates of the view that human beings are innately endowed with altruistic dispositions (Holmes, 1945; Montague, 1950). It seems that Darwin (1871, Chapter 4), too, was of the opinion that altruism had some instinctive basis in man.

    It is not unreasonable to suppose that there may be inherited dispositions to behave, or to learn to behave, in ways which favor the survival of other members of a species. Nor is it inconceivable that some of the bahavior patterns of the higher animals, such as grooming or retrieval of the young, might be primitive forerunners of the altruism that is sometimes

seen in human behavior. But the application of the concept of
altruism to these forms of behavior does not shed much light on
the more highly internalized altruistic acts of which human beings appear to be capable. The usefulness of a concept of altruism is lost if we simply apply it to any behavior of an animal that benefits another member of the species. We would then
have to apply the concept to the extensive grooming behavior of
many primates (DeVore, 1965), even though the grooming is recip-
rocal and is sometimes a source of edible insects for the groom-
er. Likewise, retrieval, cleaning, and other kinds of close
contact with the young may have directly experienced pleasurable (or distress-reducing) consequences for the female adults
of some species. The concept of altruism can be better employed, in reference to a distinct phenomenon, if we use criteria which restrict it to the situation in which the behavior
of one individual is shown to be controlled by either the direct observation or the cognitive representation of its consequences for another individual. Human beings may have a
unique capacity for this type of control over their behavior.
However, one would hardly want to treat altruism as being anything like a species-specific phenomenon in humans. It shows
the great variation of occurrence and form that we can only
attribute to corresponding variation in social experience.

     Aside from a few attempts to use verbal self-report as an
index of a generalized attribute or trait of altruism (Cattell
and Horowitz, 1952; Friedrichs, 1960; Turner, 1948), most of
the empirical work that might be regarded as having any rele-
vance to altruism consists of direct observation of dispositions to share possessions with peers or to extend aid to them.
The findings of a number of studies have confirmed the common
observation that children manifest such dispositions in ways
which are determined by their developmental status, by the social cues in a specific situation, and by the occurrence of
direct external reinforcement (Doland and Adelberg, 1967;
Fischer, 1963; Gottschaldt and Frühauf-Ziegler, 1958; Handlon
and Gross, 1959; Hartshorne, May, and Maller, 1929; Hartup and
Coates, 1967; Lenrow, 1965; Murphy, 1937; Rosenhan and White,
1967; Ugurel-Semin, 1952; Wolfe and Wolfe, 1939; Wright, 1942).
Similar dispositions are apparent in the action of adults when
they are given the opportunity to behave in ways which produce
beneficial consequences for another person (Berkowitz and Daniels, 1964; Berkowitz and Friedman, 1967; Darlington and Macker,
1966; Goranson and Berkowitz, 1966; Schopler and Matthews,
1965). A great many studies also have been conducted as attempts to demonstrate analogous dispositions in other primates
(Crawford, 1941; Mason, 1959; Mason and Hollis, 1962; Masserman,
Wechkin, and Terris, 1964; Miller, Banks, and Ogawa, 1963; Nis-
sen and Crawford, 1936; Yerkes and Learned, 1925). And corresponding demonstrations have been attempted with rats (Holder,
1958; Ulrich, 1967).

None of the studies which are cited above is directly ad-
dressed to the question of how either humans or animals originally acquire the kind of empathic or vicarious responsiveness
to social cues that would provide a potentially altruistic motivational base for their dispositions to share or to give aid.
Moreover, with the exception of the studies which have been
reported by Lenrow (1965) and by Rosenhan and White (1967), it
is difficult to determine the extent to which the observed behavior is under the control of altruistic expectations. It
appears almost invariably that the behavior is reinforced by
explicit rewards, is elicited by the implicit incentive of social approval, or is a cooperative effort to produce a mutually
beneficial set of outcomes for both self and other. For example, Holder (1958) found that rats could be trained to perform
acts which had the effect of aiding another rat, when both
learning and maintenance of the acts were rewarded with food.
Ulrich (1967) designed an experiment to show that rats could
be trained to cooperate in order to escape jointly experienced
electric shock. In the study that was reported by Fischer
(1963), the sharing behavior of children was continuously reinforced by material reward or verbal praise. Virtually all of
the other studies of children and human adults have been carried out under conditions in which it would not be possible to
separate the altruistic component of the observed behavior from
the subjects' expectations of social approval.
   Daniels (1967) has described an experiment with human
adults that illustrates quite well the problem of engaging an
altruistic component in cooperative or sharing behavior which
has been established by direct reward. The experiment shows
that the facilitation of cooperative behavior by large monetary
gains breaks down when the contingencies permit subjects to
take advantage of one another. Some experiments on the cooperative behavior of monkeys in feeding situations also have generated interesting examples of the difficulty of putting such
behavior on an altruistic footing, when it is no longer instrumental to the provision of food for a hungry animal. Boren
(1966) designed a paradigm in which two pairs of monkeys were
trained to a pattern of cooperative behavior such that each
animal's operation of its own lever would produce food only for
the other. The monkeys were permitted visual, auditory, and
tactile contact, and therefore had available the social cues
for empathic or vicarious experience. Mutual exchange behavior
was stable under the constraints of an alternation procedure
which made it highly probable that each monkey would eat and
press the lever intermittently. The exchange soon deteriorated,
however, when the monkeys were shifted to a free-responding situation which made it more likely that either monkey could con-
tinually receive food without pressing its own lever. Horel,
Treichler, and Meyer (1963) found that it was extremely diffi-

cult for the hungry member of a pair of monkeys to induce its
already satiated mate to perform previously learned behavior
that would produce food for the hungry monkey, even though the
hungry monkey was the dominant member of the pair. It appeared
that the hungry monkey had to use some coercion and direct physical guidance in order to induce the satiated monkey to perform the required behavior.

Experiments which have focussed on the reactions which
monkeys show to the distress of others are equally difficult to
interpret as demonstrations of altruism. For example, R. E.
Miller and his collaborators (Miller *et al.*, 1963; Miller,
Caul, and Mirsky, 1967) first have trained monkeys to avoid
shock in response to nonsocial cues, and then have observed
that one monkey will respond to the distress cues of another in
order to avoid shock to both itself and the other. Masserman
et al. (1964) found that monkeys would suppress the act of pulling a chain if it produced visible distress (through electric
shock) in another monkey, even though the same act also produced food for themselves. But their monkeys also could obtain
food by pulling another chain that did not produce distress in
another monkey. Both of these types of experiments demonstrate
the point that the altruistic character of an act remains indeterminate unless the performance of the act can be shown to be
empathically or vicariously controlled by its consequences for
others. The experiments were designed in such a way that the
subjects might have been acting to avoid stimulation (either
shock or distress cues) which they experienced as directly
aversive to themselves.

A comparison of the findings of two closely related experiments with rats is a particularly instructive confirmation of
the fact that acts which reduce another individual's distress
need not be empathically or vicariously motivated, but may
rather be controlled by the directly aversive properties of the
distress cues for the observer. Rice and Gainer (1962) found
that rats would press a bar in order to lower a suspended and
distressed peer significantly more often than they would press
a bar in order to lower a plastic block. But Lavery and Foley
(1963) showed that the bar-pressing behavior appeared to be
comparably reinforced by the termination of white noise and by
the termination of recorded distress squeals. Clearly, the
rats in the earlier experiment might not have been reacting
empathically to cues which they perceived as signals of another animal's distress, but might rather have been reacting to
their own directly aversive experience of the distress cues.
In a later experiment, Rice (1964) did in fact find that rats
showed evidence of fear in response to the observed distress of
a peer, even when they were exposed only to recorded squeals of
distress. These findings are similar to an informal observation that was made some years ago by Lorenz (1934), who noted

that a jackdaw was as likely to attack him if he were holding
a wet black bathing suit as it was if he were holding another
jackdaw.

One way of demonstrating the learning of altruistic behavior is suggested in an experiment that has been conducted by
the author with the collaboration of Vivian Paskal (Aronfreed
and Paskal, 1965). Six- to eight-year-old girls and an adult
female agent of socialization were used in the experiment. The
experiment was designed first to attach the child's empathic
positive affect to cues which expressed a corresponding affective state of the agent, and then to establish the altruistic
value of an overt act that the child could use instrumentally
to produce the agent's expressive cues. During the initial socialization paradigms, the agent sat very close to the child
and demonstrated the operation of a choice box that was auto-
mated to dispense a small candy as the outcome of the operation
of one lever and a three-second-red light as the outcome of the
operation c⁵ another lever. Each outcome was programmed, however, only to a randomized sixty per cent schedule, so that the
occurrence of an outcome would be unpredictable on any single
trial. During the demonstration, the child simply watched
while the agent varied her choices equally between the two
levers over the course of twenty trials. The agent showed no
reaction when her choices produced no explicit outcomes. Nor
did she show any reaction when her choices produced candy. But
when the agent's choices activated the red light, she showed
one of three patterns of reaction which represented variations
in the contingencies between her expressive cues and her behavior toward the child. These variations were designed to support the inference that the reinforcement value of the expressive cues, when they were used as outcomes of the child's own
subsequent choices among alternative acts, was attributable to
their conditioned elicitation of the child's empathic affective
experience.

In the basic experimental paradigm, the children were exposed repeatedly to a very close temporal association between
the agent's expressive cues of pleasure and their own direct
experience of the agent's physical affection. Whenever the
agent's choice between the levers activated the red light, the
agent smiled while staring at the light, and at the same time
uttered one of four exclamations in a pleased and excited tone
of voice. All of the exclamations were roughly equivalent to:
"*There's the light*!" Immediately following these expressive
cues, the agent used one arm to give the child a firm hug, and
simultaneously turned toward the child and inclined her head
with a very broad direct smile. This affection was dispensed
as though it were the spontaneous correlate of the agent's
pleasurable reaction to the red light. Children in one control
paradigm were exposed only to the agent's expressive affective

cues, while children in another control paradigm were exposed only to the agent's affection.[1]

The effects of the three paradigms were then immediately tested in a common performance task, during which the child herself operated the choice box over a great many trials. The red light on the face of the box, which originally had served as a potential outcome of the agent's choices, was now deactivated on a pretext. The agent sat across from the child, facing the rear of the box, with her gaze fixed on another red light that was visible only to her. The presence of this auxiliary light was made known to the child, who was told that it would go on whenever she chose the light-producing lever., The child was also told that she could keep all of the candy that came out of the box (although it was not to be consumed until the task was completed). During the task, the agent showed no reaction when the child chose to produce candy for herself. But whenever the child chose to operate the lever which produced the red light, the agent would smile at the light and exclaim *"There's the light!"*. She thus emitted the same expressive cues which had been used to convey her pleasure in two of the three initial paradigms. The performance task placed the child, then, in a situation where her empathic and altruistic dispositions could be tested by her repeated choices between an act that produced candy for herself and an act that produced only observably pleasurable consequences for another person.

The conjunction of the expressive cues of the agent with the child's direct experience of affection, during the basic experimental paradigm for empathic conditioning, had a substantial effect on the children's choices during the test for altruism. Children who were exposed to this conjunction were significantly more willing to forego candy than were children whose earlier experience had included only an association between the red light and the agent's expressive cues of positive affect (without physical affection). They also showed significantly more altruism than did children who previously had been exposed only to physical affection in association with the red light (without the compound of expressive affective cues that was used by the agent during the test task). The majority of the children who had been exposed to the basic social conditioning paradigm actually chose to produce the light for the agent more frequently than they chose to produce candy for themselves;

[1]Fifty-seven girls were used in the basic experimental paradigm. Thirty-seven girls were used in the control paradigm in which no physical affection was given to the child. Thirty-one girls were used in the control paradigm in which the agent did not emit expressive affective cues in response to the light.

whereas children from both of the control groups typically chose the candy-producing lever more frequently. In accordance with a distinction that was made earlier, it would appear that the altruistic behavior of the children in the experimental group was reinforced through empathic experience, but that it might also have been partially supported by vicarious experience. The children were able to see the agent's expressive affective cues during the test, but they were also able to see cues which indicated the agent's orientation toward maximizing her perception of the red light (for example, staring at the light).

The procedures which were used to establish and demonstrate the value of the agent's affective cues, for the children in the basic experimental group, were a specific application of a more general sequence of procedures that has been used in other settings to establish and test the acquired positive reinforcement value of a "neutral" stimulus. In this case, the expressive cues and the child's direct experience of affection were paired within the contingencies of a Pavlovian conditioning paradigm, during which the child was an observer—that is, the pairing was not contingent on the child's performance of a criterial overt act. The findings of a number of experiments with animals appear to confirm that the positive secondary reinforcement value of a stimulus can be acquired under Pavlovian contingencies which do not require the pairing with an unconditioned stimulus to be produced by the subject's overt behavior (Ferster and Skinner, 1957; Kelleher and Gollub, 1962; Knott and Clayton, 1966; Stein, 1958). But the distinguishing feature of the index of secondary reinforcement value which was used in the performance test for altruism was that it employed expressive cues which apparently had acquired empathic affective value for the children in the conditioning group.

The contingencies within the three initial paradigms, and their relationship to the contingencies of the performance test, were constructed with the intent of eliminating the possibility that differences among the groups in their test behavior could be attributed to differences in the children's perception of the agent's expressive cues as approval of their choices. Since the agent's affective cues were not contingent on the children's overt behavior during the initial paradigms, but were made contingent on the overt choices of all groups during the test, the experimental effect cannot easily be attributed to the children's perception of the cues as evidence of direct social approval. Finally, it is interesting to note that the effectiveness of the agent's cues of pleasurable affect, in the reinforcement of the altruistic choices of children in the experimental group, appeared to be as great during the second half of the test trials as during the first half. The apparent resistance to extinction of the value of the expressive cues

might have been partly attributable to the inconsistent scheduling of both the cues and the agent's affection, with respect
to the choices on which these events were contingent during the
conditioning and test situations. The findings of other experiments with children suggest that the independent maintenance of
the acquired positive secondary reinforcement value of a stimulus event can be prolonged by inconsistent scheduling of the
event during extinction, and that it also can be enhanced by an
original association of the event with a "primary" event that
was used as an inconsistent outcome during acquisition (Myers
and Myers, 1963; Myers, 1960; Myers and Myers, 1966).

Midlarsky and Bryan (1967) recently have reported an interesting replication and extension of this experimental demonstration of the socialization of altruism. Using essentially
the same conditioning and control paradigms as those which already have been described, they also included two additional
paradigms. One of these additional paradigms used a backward
conditioning sequence, in which the agent's physical affection
toward the child preceded her expressive cues of pleasurable
affect. The other additional paradigm was a control paradigm
in which neither expressive cues nor physical affection was associated with the appearance of the light. In the subsequent
task that was employed as a test for altruism, only half of the
children from each of the initial paradigms were provided with
the agent's expressive cues as the outcome of choices which
they previously had observed to be associated with the occurrence of the light. The other half of the children produced no
reaction from the agent when they made such choices. During
the performance test, children from both the forward and backward conditioning paradigms more frequently made the choice
with which the agent originally had produced the light than did
children from any of the control paradigms. Thus, the two
groups for whom the agent's positive affective cues and physical affection had initially been paired, as contingent outcomes
of a light-producing choice, were the ones who were most inclined to repeat that same choice when they had an opportunity
to do so, and thereby to forego an alternative choice that
would have produced candy for themselves. A second interesting
finding was that the effect of the conditioning paradigms was
markedly facilitated by the agent's expressive cues of pleasure
in response to the children's altruistic choices during the
test, but was also apparent when the agent did not display the
expressive cues.

Midlarsky and Bryan interpret their findings as a discon-
firmation of the view that the socialization of altruism requires empathic or vicarious experience to act as a medium of
reinforcement. On the basis of the altruistic test behavior of
the children from their backward conditioning paradigm, they
argue first that contingencies of the type that would condition

acquired reinforcement value were not required in order for the
agent's expressive cues to support the child's altruistic behavior.   This argument rests on the untenable assumption that
the expressive cues could not acquire additional positive value
for the child if they followed rather than preceded the child's
experience of physical affection.   Although there is considerable question about the conditions under which backward conditioning occurs (Kimble, 1961), there is also a large body of
evidence that points to the reality of the phenomenon (Razran,
1956).   Backward conditioning might be especially viable when
physical affection and expressive affective cues are blended
together in close succession in the experience of a highly
cognitive organism—particularly in view of the possibility
that the positive affectivity which is aroused by a quick hug
may reach its highest magnitude after the hug is terminated.

Secondly, Midlarsky and Bryan argue that contiguity between expressive cues and physical affection was not a crucial
determinant of their experimental effects, on the grounds that
the effects remained constant across the test trials regardless
of whether or not the agent's expressive cues were used as a
reinforcing outcome of the child's altruistic choices.   But
their own evidence would appear to contradict this argument.
The effects of the conditioning paradigms were significantly
greater when expressive cues were used during the test than
they were when the cues were not used.   Moreover, children who
had been exposed only to expressive cues during the demonstration paradigm did not show the high level of altruism that
characterized the behavior of the conditioning groups during
the test.   It is hardly surprising that a distinct effect of
the conditioning paradigms would be apparent even in the absence of any concrete expressive cues from the agent during the
test.   One would certainly expect that the acquired positive
value of the cues, and their consequent empathic reinforcing
properties, could operate through the child's capacity to give
them a cognitive representation whenever it made an altruistic
choice.

Midlarsky and Bryan used a second test of altruism which
also indicated that the agent's expressive cues had acquired
empathic reinforcement value during their conditioning paradigms.   Immediately at the end of the first test, all of the
children were equated on the number of candies which they possessed, and then were given the opportunity to make an anony-
mous donation of some of their candy to a fictitious unfortunate child.   Children who had been exposed to the original
conditioning paradigms were significantly more altruistic than
children who had been exposed to the control paradigms, but
only when the agent's expressive cues had been used as reinforcing outcomes of the child's altruistic choices during the
first test.   This finding leaves little doubt that the expres-

sive cues did acquire some empathic value as a result of conditioning. Their reinforcing properties during the first test were an effective determinant of the children's generalization of altruistic dispositions to the second test. The fact that the generalization took place across rather different situations, and was not dependent on the presence of the original object of altruism, suggests also that the altruistic behavior of these children was under the internalized control of their cognitive representations of the consequences of their actions for others.

In the type of experiment that has been described here, the value of an altruistic act is established for the child by providing a situation in which the act will be performed and then reinforced by an outcome that can elicit the child's empathic affective response. The more general paradigm for the acquisition of an altruistic component of behavior consists of two basic prerequisites: first, the attachment of potentially reinforcing empathic or vicarious changes of affectivity to social cues which transmit information about the experience of others; second, the establishment of the instrumental value of overt acts for which such social cues are contingent outcomes—initially through their external occurrence as visible indicators of the experience of others, and subsequently through their cognitive representation by the child. The acquired behavioral form of an altruistic disposition does not require, however, a repeated performance by the child under the control of reinforcing outcomes. Altruistic acts also often may be acquired by imitative modelling or by related forms of learning which utilize the child's observation of the behavior of others and its capacity to store the information that is transmitted in the consequences of their behavior. . . .

Thomas Nagel

THE POSSIBILITY OF ALTRUISM

From *The Possibility of Altruism* (Oxford: Clarendon Press, 1970), chap. 9 and section 2 of chap. 13, pp. 79–89, 127–28. Reprinted here by permission of The Clarendon Press, Oxford. It is hoped that the reader will be able to understand this selection sufficiently well to be struck by the intuitive plausibility of Nagel's conception of altruism, even without having read the parts of Nagel's book that precede chapter 9. A fuller appreciation of this selection, however, would require a reading of Nagel's book in its entirety; and the reader who finds himself intrigued by this selection will find that enterprise very worthwhile. Thomas Nagel is associate professor of philosophy at Princeton University and is also an associate editor of *Philosophy and Public Affairs*. He has published a number of articles on ethics and the philosophy of mind.

1. The problem of how, if at all, altruism is possible has much in common with the corresponding problem about prudence. By altruism I mean not abject self-sacrifice, but merely a willingness to act in consideration of the interests of other persons, without the need of ulterior motives.[1] How is it possible that such considerations should motivate us at all? What sort of system, and what further intervening factors, are necessary in order to justify and to explain behaviour which has as its object the benefit of others? (As in the case of prudence, the problem can be treated without attempting to provide too fine an analysis of benefit and harm, happiness, unhappiness, pleasure, pain, or whatever the principal determinants, positive and negative, are to be. The question is not why these particular factors motivate, but how, given that they motivate in one way, they can also motivate in another—over time or across the gap between persons.)

The problem at this stage is not how the interests of others can motivate us to some specific policy of altruistic conduct, but how they can motivate us at all. Obviously *some* account of such behaviour is needed by most ethical theories, since there are few which do not include some requirements of other-regarding action. Even if the required social behaviour does not include serious self-sacrifice, it will almost certainly include cases in which no obviously self-interested motive is present, and in which some inconvenience or at least no benefit to the agent is likely to result. A defence of altruism in terms of self-interest is therefore unlikely to be successful. But there are other interests to which appeal may be made, including the indiscriminate general sentiments of sympathy or benevolence.

It is possible to argue against such hypotheses on the ground that the psychological and societal principles to which

---

[1]I shall put aside for the time being all questions about the relative weight to be assigned to the interests of oneself and others, in a system of reasons which can qualify as altruistic.

they appeal are neither universal nor obvious enough to account for the extent of altruistic motivation, and that they are evidently false to the phenomena.[2] However, I prefer to concentrate instead on trying to provide a better account, thereby showing that an appeal to our interests or sentiments, to account for altruism, is superfluous. My general reply to such suggestions is that without question people may be motivated by benevolence, sympathy, love, redirected self-interest, and various other influences, on some of the occasions on which they pursue the interests of others, but that there is also something else, a motivation available when none of those are, and also operative when they are present, which has genuinely the status of a rational requirement on human conduct. There is in other words such a thing as pure altruism (though it may never occur in isolation from all other motives). It is the direct influence of one person's interest on the actions of another, simply because in itself the interest of the former provides the latter with a reason to act. If any further internal factor can be said to interact with the external circumstances in such a case, it will be not a desire or an inclination but the structure represented by such a system of reasons.

A suggestion of this sort will have to deal with opposition similar to that evoked by the corresponding thesis about prudential motives. With regard to prudence, we had to contend with the intuition that since even when preparing for the future I am acting in the present, it must be a present reason which motivates me, something which I want *now*. With regard to altruism, the corresponding intuition is that since it is I who am acting, even when I act in the interests of another, it must be an interest of mine which provides the impulse. If so, any convincing justification of apparently altruistic behaviour must appeal to what I want.

[2]There is one common account which can perhaps be disposed of here; the view that other-regarding behaviour is motivated by a desire to avoid the guilt feelings which would result from selfish behaviour. Guilt cannot provide the basic reason, because guilt is precisely the pained recognition that one is acting or has acted contrary to a reason which the claims, rights, or interests of others provide—a reason which must therefore be antecedently acknowledged.

Let me add that a similar argument can be given against appeals to a generalized sympathy as the basis of moral motivations. Sympathy is not, in general, just a feeling of discomfort produced by the recognition of distress in others, which in turn motivates one to relieve their distress. Rather, it is the pained awareness of their distress *as something to be relieved*.

The same prejudices are in operation here which have been observed to influence discussions of prudence: the conviction that every motivation must conform to the model of an inner force; the view that behind every motivated action lies a desire which provides the active energy for it; the assumption that to provide a justification capable also of *explaining* action, an appropriate motivation, usually a desire, must be among the conditions of the justification. If, as seems unavoidable, we are to explain the influence on a person of factors external to him in terms of their interaction with something internal to him, it is natural to assume that a desire, which can take the good of others directly or indirectly as its object, must provide the motivational force behind altruistic conduct. Bluntly: the belief that an act of mine will benefit someone else can motivate me only because I want his good, or else want something which involves it.[3]

The general assumptions behind such a view have been criticized at length in Chapter V, and I do not propose to repeat those criticisms here, for they apply without significant variation and with equal validity to the present employment of these assumptions. Briefly: in so far as a desire must be present if I am motivated to act in the interest of another, it need not be a desire of the sort which can form the *basis* for a motivation. It may, instead, be a desire which is itself motivated by reasons which the other person's interests provide. And if that is so, it cannot be among the conditions for the presence of such reasons. Desire is not the only possible source of motivation. Therefore we may look for other internal factors which connect belief and action in the altruistic case. Instead of ending the explanation with an altruistic desire which is simply postulated, we can do better by inquiring how such desires are possible, and what in our nature makes us capable of wanting other people's happiness or well-being.

The account I offer will depend on a formal feature of practical reasoning which has a metaphysical explanation.

Alternative hypotheses fail as plausible candidates for a complete account of altruistic action because none of them provides the type of simple, absolute generality which is required.

---

[3]The bluntness of this position may be modified, however, by the observation that it permits a distinction between selfish and unselfish behaviour. If what I want is genuinely another's happiness, the object of my actions may simply *be* his happiness, rather than the satisfaction of my own desire for it. This point was made by Joseph Butler long ago, in opposition to the claim that all action is motivated by self-love; *Fifteen Sermons Preached at the Rolls Chapel* (London, 1726), esp. Sermon XI, 'Upon the Love of Our Neighbor'.

There is a considerateness for others which is beyond the reach
of complicated reflections about social advantage, and which
does not require the operation of any specific sentiment. The
task is to discover an account of this general, passionless motivation which will make its existence plausible. Introspec-
tive and empirical investigation are not very useful in this
area since the motivation is often partly or completely blocked
in its operation by the interference of corrupting factors: re-
pression, rationalization, blindness, weakness. Arguments and
theoretical considerations can, however, reveal the form of an
altruistic *component* in practical reason, which will be one
contribution among others to the genesis of action.

2. The rational altruism which I shall defend can be in-
tuitively represented by the familiar argument, 'How would you
like it if someone did that to you?' It is an argument to
which we are all in some degree susceptible; but how it works,
how it can be persuasive, is a matter of controversy. We may
assume that the situation in which it is offered is one in
which you would not like it if another person did to you what
you are doing to someone now (the formula can be changed depending on the type of case; it can probably be used, if it
works at all, to persuade people to help others as well as to
avoid hurting them). But what follows from this? If no one *is*
doing it to you, how can your conduct be influenced by the hypothetical admission that if someone were, you would not like
it?

Various hypotheses suggest themselves. It could be that
you are afraid that your present behaviour will have the result
that someone *will* do the same to you; your behaviour might
bring this about either directly or through the encouragement
of a general practice of some kind. It could be that the
thought of yourself in a position similar to that of your victim is so vivid and unpleasant that you find it distasteful to
go on persecuting the wretch. But what if you have neither
this belief nor this degree of affective response? Or alterna-
tively, why cannot such considerations motivate you to increase
your security against retaliation, or take a tranquillizer to
quell your pity, rather than to desist from your persecutions?

There is something else to the argument; it does not appeal solely to the passions, but is a genuine argument whose
conclusion is a judgment. The essential fact is that you would
not only *dislike* it if someone else treated you in that way;
you would resent it. That is, you would think that your plight
gave the other person a reason to terminate or modify his contribution to it, and that in failing to do so he was acting
contrary to reasons which were plainly available to him. In
other words, the argument appeals to a *judgment* that you would
make in the hypothetical case, a judgment applying a general
principle which is relevant to the present case as well. It is

a question not of compassion but of simply connecting, in order to see what one's attitudes commit one to.

Recognition of the other person's reality, and the possibility of putting yourself in his place, is essential. You see the present situation as a specimen of a more general scheme, in which the characters can be exchanged. The crucial factor injected into this scheme is an attitude which you have towards your own case, or rather an aspect of the view which you take of your own needs, actions, and desires. You attribute to them, in fact, a certain objective interest, and the recognition of others as persons like yourself permits extension of this objective interest to the needs and desires of persons in general, or to those of any particular individual whose situation is being considered. That is accomplished by the schematic argument. But the initial intuition in your own case is what must be investigated.

It is important that the reasons which you believe others have to consider your interests, should not refer to them specifically as *yours*. That is, you must be prepared to grant that if you were in the position in question, other people would have as their reason to help you simply that *someone* was in need of help. Otherwise there would be no way of concluding from the presence of such reasons in the event that you needed help to the presence of similar reasons in the present case, when someone else is in the unfortunate situation and you are in a position to help him. So to explain how the argument works, we must discover an aspect of your attitude towards your own needs, desires, and interests which permits you to regard them as worthy of consideration simply as *someone's* needs, desires, and interests, rather than as yours.

If there actually is such an attitude, then the form of the intuitive argument we have been considering is not really essential—since it will be possible to bring that attitude to bear on the needs, desires and interests of another person directly. His interests are *someone's* interests as much as yours are. However, the argument at least reveals the connection between attitudes towards your own and towards other cases, and allows us to focus our analysis on attitudes of the former type, which are more vivid and require less imaginative effort. If one's sense of the reality of other persons is already sufficiently vivid, the argument may be superfluous; but since most of us are in varying degrees blind to other people, it is useful to be asked to imagine ourselves in their place, thus appealing to an objective element in the concern we feel for ourselves, and generalizing from that.

I shall therefore concentrate on each person's practical and evaluative judgments about his own needs, etc.; especially the relation between the reasons they give him to act because they are *his* needs, and the reasons he thinks they provide for

others to act, simply because they are *someone's* needs. Our
primary task will be to discover a foundation for the latter
belief.

   3. The primary opposition to my view comes from egoism, a
general position which corresponds in this controversy to the
preference of dated to timeless reasons in the controversy over
prudence. Egoism holds that each individual's reasons for acting and possible motivations for acting, must arise from his
own interests and desires, however those interests may be defined. The interests of one person can on this view motivate
another or provide him with a reason only if they are connected
with his interests or are objects of some sentiment of his,
like sympathy, pity, or benevolence.

   Those who occupy this philosophical position may believe
that they are, as a matter of psychological fact, egoists, but
I doubt that there are any genuine specimens of the type. It
should be noticed how peculiar egoism would be in practice; it
would have to show itself not only in the lack of a direct concern for others but also in an inability to regard one's own
concerns as being of interest to anyone else, except instrumentally or contingently upon the operation of some sentiment.
An egoist who needs help, before concluding that anyone else
has reason to assist him, must be able to answer the question
'What's it to him?' He is precluded from feeling resentment,
which embodies the judgment that another is failing to act on
reasons with which one's own needs provide him. No matter how
extreme his own concern the egoist will not feel that this in
itself need be of interest to anyone else. The pain which
gives him a reason to remove his gouty toes from under another
person's heel does not in itself give the other any reason to
remove the heel, since it is not his pain.

   Anyone who thinks he is an egoist should imagine himself
in either role in such a situation. Can he truly affirm that
the owner of the heel has no reason whatever to remove it from
the gouty toes? Particularly if one owns the toes, it shows a
rare detachment not to regard the pain as simply in itself a
bad thing, which there is reason for anyone to avert. It is
difficult, in other words, to resist the tendency to objectify
the negative value which one assigns to pain, or would assign
to it if one experienced it, regarding the identity of its owner as irrelevant.

   The procedure may be different for different kinds of
reasons, but the idea is the same: that in accepting goals or
reasons myself I attach objective value to certain circumstances, not just value for myself; similarly when I acknowledge that others have reason to act in their own interests,
these must finally be reasons not just for them, but objective
reasons for the goals which they pursue or the acts which they
perform.

Arguments against the coherency of ethical egoism have been offered in the past, and it may be in order to distinguish them from the one I propose to offer. The arguments with which I am familiar all focus on egoism as a universal position, and find incoherencies in the judgments which it requires a man to make about other people, and in what it requires him in general to urge or support. I wish to suggest, on the other hand, that ethical egoism is already objectionable in its application by each person to his *own* case, and to his own reasons for action. Let me mention briefly some earlier arguments.

There is the position of G. E. Moore, who claimed that egoism involves a straightforward contradiction, for it asserts 'that *each* man's happiness is the sole good—that a number of different things are *each* of them the only good thing there is —an absolute contradiction!' An egoist may be inclined to object that his view is only that each man's happiness or interest is the sole good *for him* but Moore has already disallowed this move:

> When I talk of a thing as 'my own good', all that I can mean is that something which will be exclusively mine (whatever be the various senses of this relation denoted by 'possession'), is also *good absolutely*; or rather that my possession of it is *good absolutely*. The *good* of it can in no possible sense be 'private' or belong to me; any more than a thing can *exist* privately, or *for* one person only. The only reason I can have for aiming at 'my own good', is that it is *good absolutely* that what I so call should belong to me— *good absolutely* that I should *have* something, which, if I have it, others cannot have. But if it is *good absolutely* that I should have it, then everyone else has as much reason for aiming at *my* having it, as I have myself.[4]

He goes on to say more to the same effect, but nothing resembling an argument is offered for these claims.[5] What I wish

---

[4]*Principia Ethica* (Cambridge, 1903), p. 99. Although Moore treats egoism as a theory about the good, while I treat it as a theory about reasons, the two are clearly related, since Moore believes that the good is that at which one has reason to aim. I myself do not wish to make any claims about good and bad, or about their relation to reasons for action.

[5]They seem to him self-evident because he regards it as already established that 'good' is a one-place predicate denoting a simple, non-natural property. But that would not be granted by an egoist, whose fundamental evaluative concept would be a *re-*

to explain is exactly what he assumes: that in order to accept
something as a goal for oneself, one must be able to regard its
achievement by oneself as an *objective* good.

Other arguments, such as those of Medlin[6] and Baier,[7]
point out that egoism leads to inconsistent attitudes and behaviour if, as an ethical doctrine, it is to govern not only
one's own actions but also what one wants and encourages others
to do, or what one is obliged to permit them to do. But if
these objections are correct, they leave a more fundamental
question unanswered: Why should the acceptance of a universal
principle of conduct commit one to any desires at all about the
conformity of others to that principle? Why should the judgment that another person has reason to act in certain ways provide you with *any* reason for wanting him to do so?

There is a further question: Why need one adopt *general*
principles of action at all—i.e. principles applying to others
besides oneself? Why can one not restrict oneself to the acceptance of personal principles of action—which may be con-
strued as intentions, some longer-term or more general than
others but all nevertheless applicable only to one's own behaviour? About this question something will be said later on.

It is a requirement of universality on practical principles, in a specific form which excludes most types of egoism,
that will be defended here. And it will be supported by reflections about what happens when one acts in one's own interest. That case by itself contains the basis for a challenge
to egoism.

It should be emphasized that by 'egoism' I mean the relatively narrow and specific view that the only *source* of reasons
for action lies in the interests of the agent. The term might
also be applied to a variety of other views, and I do not propose to argue against all of them. Some fall prey to the general argument which will be offered; others do not. And of the
latter, some (e.g. egoism as an instrumental policy likely to
lead to everyone's happiness if generally practised) can be

---

[5](cont.) *lation*: 'X is good for Y.' A similar criticism is made
by C. D. Broad, 'Certain Features in Moore's Ethical Doctrines',
in *The Philosophy of G. E. Moore*, ed. P. A. Schilpp (Evanston
and Chicago, 1942).

[6]Brian Medlin, 'Ultimate Principles and Ethical Egoism',
Australasian Journal of Philosophy (1957).

[7]Kurt Baier, *The Moral Point of View* (Ithaca: Cornell University
Press, 1958); abridged edition (New York: Random House, 1965),
p. 95.

refuted on empirical grounds,[8] whereas others perhaps cannot
(e.g. the view that life is like a competitive game, which it
is objectively good that everyone should play to win). More
will be said on this subject in the course of the argument.
    4. I shall attempt to explain altruism, like prudence, as
a rational requirement on action. Just as it became clear in
the earlier discussion that prudence is not fundamental, but
derives from the requirement that reasons be timelessly formu-
lable, so it will turn out that altruism is not fundamental,
but derives from something more general: a formal principle
which can be specified without mentioning the interests of
others at all. That principle will, moreover, be closely analogous to the formal principle of timelessness, in that it
will deny the possibility of restricting to one *person* the derivative influence of a reason for action, just as the formal
principle which underlies prudence denies the possibility of
restricting such derivative influence to one *time*. The principle underlying altruism will require, in other words, that all
reasons be construable as expressing objective rather than subjective values. In both cases the relevant condition on reasons is a purely formal one, compatible with considerable variety in the content of those reasons which satisfy it. Therefore the acceptance of prudence, or of altruism, is no substitute for a general theory of value and human interests. Both
prudence and altruism impose conditions on the derivative influence of primary reasons whose sources lie elsewhere.
    The attempt to discover such a general requirement on con-
duct as I have described, and to provide a plausible interpretation of it, is indebted to the earlier efforts to defend prudence. Not only the general enterprise, but also the form of
the present principle and the method of interpretation will
parallel those of the earlier case. Specifically, it will be
argued that the condition of *objectivity* (as I shall call it)
is the practical expression of a conception possessed by any
rational, acting subject, though not in this case the conception of himself as temporally extended. As has been indicated
in Ch. IV, §I, the conception underlying altruism is that of
oneself as merely one person among others, and of others as
persons in just as full a sense. This is parallel to the central element in a conception of oneself as temporally extended:
that the present is just a time among others, and that other
times are equally real. As we shall see, the two views have
similar analyses and parallel consequences.

[8]On the other hand, if an instrumental egoism should be supported by *true* empirical premises, it need not conflict with
altruism. If in fact egoistic conduct is the best means to
the general happiness, then altruism probably requires it.
But that is not the egoism that I am talking about.

My argument is intended to demonstrate that altruism (or its parent principle) depends on a full recognition of the reality of other persons. Nevertheless the central conception in my proposed interpretation will be a conception of *oneself*, and the argument will rest on an analysis of how this conception bears on self-interested action. This method is allowable, because recognition of the reality of others depends on a conception of oneself, just as recognition of the reality of the future depends on a conception of the present.[9]

The precise form of altruism which derives from this argument will depend on a further factor, namely the nature of the primary reasons for action which individuals possess. If these are tied to the pursuit of their interests, in some ordinary sense of that term, then a normal requirement of altruism will be the result. But if the general reasons with which we begin are not tied to individual goals, the resulting objective system may require the common pursuit of certain goals without involving altruism in the usual sense at all, i.e. concern for the needs and interests of other individuals.

It is not at all obvious what our interests are, let alone what part they play in determining reasons for our conduct. I doubt, for one thing, that the satisfaction of basic desires comes anywhere near to exhausting the notion of interest. Moreover, there may be values which have nothing to do with interests at all. I do not in fact possess a general theory of the values to be embodied in a catalogue of primary reasons, but I am fairly certain that they are complicated enough to ensure that even if the formal result defended here is correct, what will emerge from it is neither utilitarianism, nor any other moral system which is simply altruistic. . . .

. . . . The possibility of simple altruism depends on acknowledgment of a special type of subjective reason, and its submission to the procedure of objectification. The relevant subjective reasons are those which attach to the satisfaction of certain of one's needs and interests *per se*, without too much concern over the source of that satisfaction.

---

[9]In fact, since altruism is in a sense a hypothetical principle, stating what one has reason to do *if* what one does will affect the interests of others, it could be accepted even by someone who believed that there were no other people. Without believing in their actual existence, he could still believe in the reality of other persons in the sense that he might regard himself as a type of individual of which there could be other specimens, as real as he was. The source of this hypothetical altruism towards these possible other beings would lie in the connection between the conception of himself which allowed him to believe in their possibility, and his own self-interested concerns.

This is by no means true of all interests, and the character of an objective principle depends to a great extent on the character of the subjective reason from which it derives. If the proper ends of human life are understood in a sufficiently eccentric fashion, their objective correlates may be equally eccentric. For example, the condition of objectivity could be met by principles of conduct which demanded the fiercest self-reliance and competitiveness of all individuals, positively forbidding them either to assist each other or to accept assistance in overcoming difficulty, and enjoining them only to continue the struggle for survival or domination, and to see that others continued it as well. Such a position would follow from the objectification of a view of individual interest which made struggle, competition, and danger the primary subjective goals.[10]

But not all reasons are so involuted. At least sometimes objectification will demand that everyone pursue an uncomplicated end which we already acknowledge a subjective reason to pursue; the elimination of pain, for example, or survival, or the satisfaction of basic appetites. If this is the case, then we have prima facie reason to secure those ends for others as well as for ourselves. That is not to deny that there may be reasons to secure them for ourselves and those closely related to us; various factors may complicate the result when there is conflict between reasons to help others and reasons to help oneself. But even if we allow for these possibilities, the acknowledgment of prima facie reasons to help others is a significant result. It means at least this: that when one can secure or promote such an end for someone else, and either (a) there are no conflicting reasons, or (b) all other considerations balance out, then one has sufficient reason to act. The reason is *simply* that one's act will promote the other's survival, eliminate his suffering, or what have you. It depends on no desire or interest of the agent—only on the objectivity of certain reasons which he acknowledges subjectively. This is a non-trivial result (however rarely the circumstances described may be thought to arise), and an acceptable one. It is neither paradoxical nor counter-intuitive to maintain that one automatically has a reason to help someone in need if there is no reason not to. . . .

---

[10]A caricature of Nietzsche's position might take such a form, and that is instructive in one respect: it suggests that he is not an egoist. Such values as he admits are objective rather than subjective.

Bibliography

Textbooks

For introductory discussions of both psychological and
ethical egoism, the reader is invited to consult the following:

Brandt, Richard B. *Ethical Theory*. Englewood Cliffs,
  N.J.: Prentice-Hall, 1959. Pp. 307-14, 369-78.
Frankena, William K. *Ethics*. Englewood Cliffs, N.J.:
  Prentice-Hall, 1963. Chap. 2.
Hospers, John. *Human Conduct*. New York: Harcourt
  Brace Jovanovich, 1961. Chap. 4.

Historical Writings

In addition to the works of the historical figures whose
writings appear in this volume, the reader may wish to consult
the following:

Aristotle. *Nicomachean Ethics*.
Hutcheson, Francis. *An Enquiry Concerning Moral Good
  and Evil*. 1729.
Mandeville, Bernard. *The Fable of the Bees*. 1723.
Plato. *Meno, Protagoras*, and *Republic*.

Psychological Egoism

The following books and articles are primarily relevant to
the topic of psychological egoism, although some of them are
relevant to ethical egoism as well:

Allport, G. W. "The Functional Autonomy of Motives."
  American Journal of Psychology 50 (1937).

Broad, C. D. *Five Types of Ethical Theory*. London:
    Routledge and Kegan Paul, 1956.
Duncker, Karl. "Pleasure, Emotion, and Striving."
    Philosophy and Phenomenological Research 1 (1940).
Nowell-Smith, P. H. *Ethics*. Baltimore, Md.: Penguin
    Books, 1954. Chap. 10.
Peters, R. S. *The Concept of Motivation*. London:
    Routledge and Kegan Paul, 1958.
Sharp, Frank C. *Ethics*. New York: Century Co., 1928.
    Chaps. 5, 22, and 23.
Sidgwick, Henry. *The Methods of Ethics*. Books 1 and
    2. New York: Macmillan Co., 1874.
Tolman, E. C. "The Determiners of Behavior at a
    Choice Point." *Psychological Review* 45 (1938).
Young, P. T. "The Role of Hedonic Processes in the
    Organization of Behavior." *Psychological Review*
    59 (1952).

Ethical Egoism

The following books and articles are primarily relevant to
the topic of ethical egoism, although, here again, some of the
works contain discussions of psychological egoism as well:

Baier, Kurt. *The Moral Point of View*. Ithaca, N.Y.:
    Cornell University Press, 1958. Chap. 8.
Brunton, J. A. "Egoism and Morality." *Philosophical
    Quarterly* 6 (1956).
Ewing, A. C. *Ethics*. New York: Collier Books, 1962.
    Chap. 2.
Gauthier, David P. *Morality and Rational Self-Inter-
    est*. Englewood Cliffs, N.J.: Prentice-Hall, 1970.
Hospers, John. "Baier and Medlin on Ethical Egoism."
    Philosophical Studies 12 (1961).
Medlin, Brian. "Ultimate Principles and Ethical
    Egoism." *Australasian Journal of Philosophy* 35
    (1957).
Moore, G. E. *Principia Ethica*. New York: Cambridge
    University Press, 1959. Pp. 96-105.
Nielsen, Kai. "Egoism in Ethics." *Philosophy and
    Phenomenological Research* 19 (1959).
Prichard, H. A. *Duty and Interest*. Oxford: Clarendon
    Press, 1928.
_____. *Moral Obligation*. Oxford: Clarendon Press,
    1949.

Empirical Investigations of Altruism

The following books and articles will introduce the reader to some of the scientific investigations of the nature of altruistic behavior carried on by psychologists and sociologists:

Bryan, J. H., and London, P. "Altruistic Behavior by Children." *Psychological Bulletin* 73 (1970).

Campbell, D. T. "Ethnocentric and Other Altruistic Motives." In D. Levine, ed., *Nebraska Symposium on Motivation*, vol. 13. Lincoln, Neb.: University of Nebraska Press, 1965.

Friedrichs, R. W. "Alter Versus Ego: An Exploratory Assessment of Altruism." *American Sociological Review* 25 (1960).

Kaufmann, Harry. *Aggression and Altruism*. New York: Holt, Rinehart and Winston, 1970.

Krebs, D. L. "Altruism: An Examination of the Concept and a Review of the Literature." *Psychological Bulletin* 73 (1970).

London, P., and Bower, R. K. "Altruism, Extroversion, and Mental Illness." *Journal of Social Psychology* 76 (1968).

Macaulay, J., and Berkowitz, L., eds. *Altruism and Helping Behavior*. New York: Academic Press, 1970.

Wright, Derek. *The Psychology of Moral Behavior*. Baltimore, Md.: Penguin Books, 1971. Chap. 6.

Basic Problems in Philosophy Series

A. I. Melden and Stanley Munsat
University of California, Irvine
General Editors

Ethical Relativism
John Ladd

Introduction   Custom Is King, *Herodotus*   Ethics and Law: Eternal Truths, *Friedrich Engels*   Folkways, *William Graham Sumner*
The Meaning of Right, *W. D. Ross*   Ethical Relativity? *Karl Duncker*   Cultural Relativism and Cultural Values, *Melville J. Herskovits*   Ethical Relativity: Sic et Non, *Clyde Kluckhohn*
Social Science and Ethical Relativism, *Paul W. Taylor*   The Issue of Relativism, *John Ladd*   The Universally Human and the Culturally Variable, *Robert Redfield*   Bibliography

Human Rights
A. I. Melden

Introduction   The Second Treatise of Civil Government, Chapters 2 and 5, *John Locke*   Anarchical Fallacies, *Jeremy Bentham*
Natural Rights, *Margaret MacDonald*   Are There Any Natural Rights? *H.L.A. Hart*   Justice and Equality, *Gregory Vlastos*
Rights, Human Rights, and Racial Discrimination, *Richard Wasserstrom*   Persons and Punishment, *Herbert Morris*   Appendices
Bibliography

Guilt and Shame
Herbert Morris

Introduction   Stavrogin's Confession, *Fyodor Dostoyevsky*   Differentiation of German Guilt, *Karl Jaspers*   Origin of the Sense of Guilt, *Sigmund Freud*   Guilt and Guilt Feelings, *Martin Buber*
Real Guilt and Neurotic Guilt, *Herbert Fingarette*   "Guilt,"
"Bad Conscience," and the Like, *Friedrich Nietzsche*   The Sense

of Justice, *John Rawls*   Shame, *Gerhart Piers* and *Milton B. Singer*   Autonomy v. Shame and Doubt, *Erik H. Erikson*   The Nature of Shame, *Helen Merrell Lynd*   Bibliography

The Analytic-Synthetic Distinction
Stanley Munsat

Introduction   First Truths, *Gottfried Wilhelm von Leibniz*   Necessary and Contingent Truths, *Gottfried Wilhelm von Leibniz*   Of Proposition, *Thomas Hobbes*   Introduction to the Critique of Pure Reason, *Immanuel Kant*   Kant, *Arthur Papp*   Of Demonstration, and Necessary Truths, *John Stuart Mill*   Views of Some Writers on the Nature of Arithmetical Propositions, *Gottlob Frege*   What Is an Empirical Science? *Bertrand Russell*   Two Dogmas of Empiricism, *Willard Van Orman Quine*   The Meaning of a Word, *John Austin*   In Defense of a Dogma, *H. P. Grice* and *P. F. Strawson*   Bibliography

Civil Disobedience and Violence
Jeffrie G. Murphy

Introduction   On Disobeying the Law, *Socrates*   On the Duty of Civil Disobedience, *Henry David Thoreau*   Legal Obligation and the Duty of Fair Play, *John Rawls*   Social Protest and Civil Obedience, *Sydney Hook*   The Vietnam War and the Right of Resistance, *Jeffrie G. Murphy*   Civil Disobedience: Prerequisite for Democracy in Mass Society, *Christian Bay*   Non-violence, *Mohandas K. Gandhi*   A Fallacy on Law and Order: That Civil Disobedience Must Be Absolutely Nonviolent, *Howard Zinn*   On Not Prosecuting Civil Disobedience, *Ronald Dworkin*   Law and Authority, *Peter Kropotkin*   Bibliography

Morality and the Law
Richard A. Wasserstrom

Introduction   On Liberty, *John Stuart Mill*   Morals and the Criminal Law, *Lord Patrick Devlin*   Immorality and Treason, *H.L.A. Hart*   Lord Devlin and the Enforcement of Morals, *Ronald Dworkin*   Sins and Crimes, *A. R. Louch*   Morals Offenses and the Model Penal Code, *Louis B. Schwartz*   Paternalism, *Gerald Dworkin*   Four cases involving the enforcement of morality   Bibliography

War and Morality
Richard A. Wasserstrom

Introduction   The Moral Equivalent of War, *William James*   The Morality of Obliteration Bombing, *John C. Ford, S.J.*   War and

Murder, *Elizabeth Anscombe*   Moral Judgment in Time of War,
Michael Walzer   Pacifism: A Philosophical Analysis, *Jan
Narveson*   On the Morality of War: A Preliminary Inquiry,
Richard Wasserstrom   Judgment and Opinion, The International
Tribunal, Nuremberg, Germany   Superior Orders, Nuclear War-
fare, and the Dictates of Conscience, *Guenter Lewy*   Selected
Bibliography